Sunday Nanosi Ndovi
Patrick Albert Chikumba

OPTMISING UNPROCESSED MILK TRANSPORTATION ROUTES IN MALAWI USING GIS

Sunday Nanosi Ndovi
Patrick Albert Chikumba

OPTMISING UNPROCESSED MILK TRANSPORTATION ROUTES IN MALAWI USING GIS

CASE STUDY OF MILK BULKING GROUPS IN THYOLO

LAP LAMBERT Academic Publishing

Cover image: www.ingimage.com

Publisher:
LAP LAMBERT Academic Publishing
is a trademark of
Dodo Books Indian Ocean Ltd. and OmniScriptum S.R.L publishing group

120 High Road, East Finchley, London, N2 9ED, United Kingdom
Str. Armeneasca 28/1, office 1, Chisinau MD-2012, Republic of Moldova, Europe
Managing Directors: Ieva Konstantinova, Victoria Ursu
info@omniscriptum.com

Printed at: see last page
ISBN: 978-620-8-42840-2

DEDICATION

I dedicate this thesis work to my wife Tumelo for being there for me throughout the entire master's program. To my daughter Katalambano and my son Keagan you were very special as you tirelessly asked me if I had worked on my thesis every day that passed. I cherish your reminders that turned into encouragement.

ACKNOWLEDGEMENTS

I offer my gratitude and appreciation to my supervisor, Dr. Patrick Albert Chikumba for the skillful ways in which you lovingly challenged and supported me throughout the whole thesis journey - knowing when to push and when to let up.

I am also thankful to Mr. Martin Bright Msendema and Dr. Kondwani Godwin Munthali for the moral and material support.

Finally, I am thankful to Chifundo Ninje for stationery and printing support throughout my course work. In addition, the stationery towards interview recording and questionnaires are worth mentioning, as I could not afford them since I was jobless at the time.

TABLE OF CONTENTS

LIST OF TABLES

LIST OF FIGURES

LIST OF ABBREVIATIONS AND ACRONYMS

1950 UTM S:	1950 Universal Traverse Mercator 1950 South
BLADD:	Blantyre Agricultural Development Division
CREMPA:	Central Region Milk Producers Association
DAHLD:	District Animal Health and Livestock Development
DAHLDO:	District Animal Health and Livestock Development Officer
DBMS:	Database Management Systems
FAMPA:	Farmers Milk Producers Association
FAO:	Food and Agriculture Organization
GDP:	Gross Domestic Product
GIS:	Geographic Information System
GoM:	Government of Malawi
GPS:	Global Positioning System
ICT:	Information and Communication Technology
JICA:	Japan International Cooperation Agency
MBG:	Milk Bulking Group
MDFA:	Mphoto Dairy Farmers Association
MGDS:	Malawi Growth and Development Strategy
MMPA:	Malawi Milk Producers Association
NSO:	National Statistics Office
NTMP:	National Transport Master Plan
NTP:	National Transport Policy
QECD:	Organization for Economic Co-operation and Development
SADC:	Southern African Development Community
SHMPA:	Shire Highlands Milk Producers Association
TDAHLDO:	Thyolo District Animal Health and Livestock Development Officer
US$:	United States Dollars
WGS84:	World Geodetic System 1984

LIST OF APPENDICES

ABSTRACT

Despite acknowledgement by the government and researchers of the importance of spatial transportation solutions in Malawi's dairy industry, the sector remains without practical solutions. Milk is a perishable food that requires timely transportation to avoid deterioration. In Malawi, smallholder dairy farmers deliver and sell milk to Milk Bulking Groups (MBGs) using various transportation modes such as foot, bicycle, and motorcycle. Milk is supplied to the MBG for bulk storage and chilling to avoid deterioration. Untimely delivery of milk results in rejection at MBG. In other instances, some farmers bypass closest MBGs for facilities located further. This worsens milk quality that is likely to be unacceptable at the milk collection center. Subsequently, these rejections lead to loss of revenue to dairy farmers. Therefore, the main objective of this study was optimizing unprocessed milk transport routes in Malawi using spatial analysis: case study of milk MBGs in Thyolo by selecting the shortest route with time as a cost attribute using Geographic Information Systems (GIS). A spatially organized transport system impedes milk deterioration while promoting profitability to farmers in the value chain. A transportation system was modelled using Spatial Autocorrelation, Buffer Analysis, Route Analysis, and Closest Facility Analysis within GIS. Thereafter, the problem was analyzed using a spatial analysis approach. Variables were tested and interpreted using quantitative and qualitative research approaches. Interviews targeted leaders from all 48 MBGs and 50 farmers from Namahoya MBG. Interviews were conducted in their natural setting and coordinates were captured in the process. Coordinates facilitated creation of maps to produce routes with least travel times. The questionnaire targeted 200 respondents. Out of the total, 182 respondents were available. The study found that farms and MBGs were randomly distributed. Furthermore, findings showed that out of the 50 sampled farmers that supplied milk to Namahoya, only 8% were nearest to the facility while 92% were closest to 9 different MBGs. Supplying milk to the nearest MBGs would reduce travel time and distance by 14.67 hours and 73.37 km respectively.

KEYWORDS: Milk, Transportation, GIS, Buffer, Route, Closest Facility

CHAPTER 1: INTRODUCTION

This chapter presents a synopsis of the topic under study by providing a broad spectrum of optimizing routes for transporting unprocessed milk from farms to milk collection centers in Malawi. Optimization of routes involved the use of Geographic Information Systems (GIS). The chapter consists of background, study area, the dairy industry in Malawi, problem statement, aim, research questions, objectives, research methods, rationale, and thesis structure.

1.1 Background

Perishable foods must be transported to the processing plant in the fastest time possible due to deterioration that is triggered by room temperature and delivery time (Abousaeidi et al. 2016). To deliver the raw food on time, one has to select the optimal route that generally reduces travel distance (Enkhtuya and Shin, 2019). Subsequently, the deterioration of foods is minimized leading to positive payoffs to stakeholders within the supply chain. To achieve timely delivery, O'Callaghan et al. (2021) assert that modelling a road network in GIS supports decision-making in selecting the shortest route.

Foods are considered perishable if they lose value over time Chaudhary et al. (2018). These foods include vegetables, fruits, meat, and fresh milk among others. Fresh milk can either be categorized as unprocessed or processed. Unprocessed fresh milk is raw milk from the udder of mammals such as cows, sheep, and goats among others. On the other hand, processed milk is raw milk that undergoes pasteurization and is later packaged and sold in food markets. This study focused on unprocessed milk that comes straight from the cow. Unprocessed cow milk is classified as a perishable food (M-Livestock Consultant, 2013).

Milk is transported between two or more geographical locations by one or mixed modes of transport to reach the destination. Literature indicates that related studies about milk transportation problems focused on milk collection between milk collection centers and processing plants. Some of these studies include those conducted by Ngigi and Wangai (2012) and Worah et al. (2012). However, this study focuses on the milk transportation problem between dairy farms and milk collection centers in Thyolo district, Malawi.

1.2 Dairy Industry in Malawi

Malawi's dairy industry is a government sub-sector that falls under the unit of animal production in the Department of Animal Health and Livestock Development (DAHLD) within the Ministry of Agriculture. In 1999 and 2003, DAHLD developed a blueprint and a strategic plan respectively where livestock activities were implemented and regulated within the framework of these strategic documents (M-Livestock Consultant, 2013). In addition to regulatory enforcement, DAHLD offers technical services such as cattle improvements, and training of dairy farmers among others.

1.2.1 Dairy Structures

The Malawian dairy industry is an important investment subsector for the Government of Malawi (Revoredo-Giha and Toma, 2016). The industry plays a vital role in the social economic development of smallholder dairy farmers by providing food, revenue, jobs, and social security (M-Livestock Consultant, 2016). Dairy contribution to the overall Gross Domestic Product was unavailable from the National Statistical Office of Malawi and other publications at the time of this investigation. This was attributed to vending of some volumes of unprocessed milk to the informal market channel than the recommended formal channel (Imani Development Consultants, 2004) rendering it problematic to even estimate. However, Chitika, (2008) reported that out of the unprocessed milk produced in a day, 19% was used for subsistence, 57% was delivered to the MBG and 23% was channeled to the informal market.

Like many other countries, Malawi has a well-organized dairy structure. It has Malawi Milk Producers Association (MMPA) as an umbrella Organization with three dairy milk sheds; Mphoto Dairy Farmers Association in the northern region, Central Region Milk Producers Association in the Central Region and Shire Highlands Milk Producers Association in the Southern region. Milk sheds have more than one Milk Bulking Groups (MBGs) as members based on geographical location. MBGs are milk facilities where more than one farmer delivers and sells milk in bulk for chilling and storage. MBGs are located within the vicinity of dairy farms and are managed by a democratically elected committee, headed by the chairperson. Then, the committee employs milk buyers, cleaners, and security personnel who run day-to-day operations. A farm is a location owned by a farmer where dairy cows are reared. The farmer supplies milk to the MBG and are categorized as large or small depending on the volumes of milk production (Revoredo-Giha, 2016).

Unprocessed milk distribution constitutes diverse buyers. These buyers are naturally positioned in different geographical locations. As a result, milk transportation covers a wide geographical area from the source to the destination. This study narrows down by primarily focusing on transportation of unprocessed cow milk from the farm to the MBG that involves smallholder dairy farmers in a rural district of Thyolo.

1.2.2 Government Role in the Milk Industry

The Government of Malawi forbids vending of raw milk to consumers due to associated health risks though it is a common practice throughout the country (Barnard, 2006). Revoredo-Giha and Toma (2016) highlight that formal and informal selling channels exist where the latter is dominant. Law of Malawi on Milk and Milk Product Act Cap. 67:05, stipulate that transportation of milk and milk products is the sole responsibility of dairy farmers, MBGs, and processors. Furthermore, it states that the Government shall not subsidize costs related to transporting. It is for this additional reason that necessitated optimization of routes using GIS in the transport network.

1.2.3 Milk Outlook

Organization for Economic Co-operation and Development; and Food and Agriculture Organization projects a 22 % increase in world milk production by 2027. 80% of the increase is expected to come from developing countries where Malawi belongs. Additional milk production will be consumed locally as fresh foods. Therefore, it is imperative to adopt GIS in the transportation of unprocessed milk so that Malawi contributes positively to the projected milk production increase. GIS-based transport model acts as a decision support system in milk deliveries.

Several studies conducted in Malawi's dairy industry have argued that there are myriad problems in the dairy industry. Some of these which are related to this study are: - (1) ineffective supply chain Revoredo-Giha et al. (2015), (2) poor quality of milk in formal channels resulting in an estimated rejection rate of 17% (ibid), (3) transport problems (Banda et al. 2011), and (4) farmers operating outside recommended 8 km radius from milk collection centers (Nyekanyeka, 2011; Revoredo-Giha et al. 2013). However, there is little evidence to show a solution and implementation to resolve the listed constraints. Therefore, this research sought to contribute solutions to aforementioned problems, particularly transport problems by optimizing routes using GIS technology.

1.3 Problem Statement

Absence of accurate traverse time and distance by smallholder dairy farmers when delivering unprocessed milk to sell at MBGs from farms. The gap results in untimely milk transportation leading to deterioration and rejection at MBG because of poor quality. In some instances, farmers traverse longer times and distances by avoiding nearest MBGs to those located further hence compromising on quality and likely denial of purchase by MBG. Consequently, these rejections draw losses in possible revenue to farmers. Therefore, this study sought to optimize routes in milk transportation between farms and MBGs using GIS. GIS determined shortest route between incidents and facilities based on the mode of transport (foot, bicycle, and motorcycle) hence functioning as a decision support system when hauling milk to the MBG.

1.4 Research Main Objective

The study aimed at optimizing routes in the transportation of unprocessed milk between the farm and the MBG using spatial methods.

1.5 Research Specific Objectives

To address the aim of the study, this research focused on 3 specific objectives: -

1. To determine problems faced by dairy farmers when delivering milk to MBG.
2. To assess spatial distribution of farms and MBGs in the study area.
3. To develop a spatial transport model to determine optimal routes using GIS.

1.6 Research Question

To achieve the aim of this study, the following is the research question:

How can rural routes be optimized when transporting unprocessed milk from farm to MBG through spatial analysis approach?

1.7 Significance of the Study

Government of Malawi positioned transportation at the top of its economic and social development agenda through Malawi Growth and Development Strategy (MGDS) III 2017- 2022, The National Transport Policy (NTP), and The Nation Transport Master Plan (NTMP) 2017-2037. MGDS III places the transport sector as one of the five key priority areas where the government intends to expand transport infrastructure to shorten distances of goods transported as imports and exports. According to JICA Malawi office 2020 report, Malawi has the poorest transport system in the SADC region which leads to high transportation charges. Regionally, transport costs average US$ 7 per tonnage for every km while in Malawi average charge ranges from US$ 7 to 10 per tonnage per km. GIS technology minimizes travel time and distance by and selecting shortest routes between incidents and facilities.

Therefore, the study explored optimization of unprocessed milk transportation routes using GIS from dairy farms to milk facilities in Thyolo district. GIS as a tool helps in calculating traverse times and distances based on mode of transport. Subsequently, finds shortest route between the farm and the milk bulking group. In proximity analysis, the tool identifies the nearest milk collection center for dairy farmers. So, incorporating GIS in unprocessed milk routes is important as it aids farmers in decision making regarding milk transportation. Mores so, avoids milk deterioration which translates into bad quality that is likely to be rejected for purchase at milk facilities.

1.8 Thesis Structure

Chapter 1 introduces subject of the thesis. It includes the research background, problem statement, aim, objectives, questions, and rationale. A literature review appears in chapter 2. It discusses relevant literature on milk transportation, spatial analysis, network analysis, and theoretical framework. Chapter 3 presents the research methodology. It comprises the study area, research approach, research design, data and material identification, sampling, data collection, ethical considerations, modelling, and limitations of the study. Chapter 4 presents the results and discussion of the study. Chapter 5 concludes the discussion and evaluates the extent to which the aim and objectives have been achieved.

CHAPTER 2: LITERATURE REVIEW AND THEORETICAL FRAMEWORK

2.1 Introduction

The chapter comprises literature on milk transportation in the dairy industry, spatial modelling and analysis, network analysis and theoretical framework. Focus is on the related literature as regards to calculation of time and distance between two or more spatial locations using GIS. In addition, the chapter also discusses how to find the nearest MBG from the farm.

2.2 Milk transportation in Dairy Industry

The section reviews GIS-based transportation of milk in both developed and developing countries. In this study, developed countries consist of China, India, Ireland and Sweden while developing countries include Mongolia, Indonesia, Tanzania, Uganda and Malawi. The study is carried out in Malawi, therefore, rigorous review of milk transportation is presented for the country.

Computer based technologies have the potential to transform smallholder farming systems into gainful business (Ali, 2012). Integration of Information and Communication Technology (ICT) in subsistence dairy farming enables conveyance of timely information for making informed decisions (Ommani & Chizari, 2008). The timely deliverance of information through computers and mobile phones provides a productive way of decision-making.

From China, a research concludes that locations, road network and other related information mapped on GIS facilitated monitoring of costs in the distribution area (Xu, 2005). The paper further argues that the GIS design finds optimal routes by using a heuristic algorithm. Not only did the results show support in decision making but also reduction in distribution expenses. In relation to this study, one of the deliverables is to model a transport system where farmers should be able to make decisions by selecting the quickest route(s) from the farms to the MBG(s).

A study by Kumar et al. (2012) in India reveals that introduction of GIS in the dairy industry is beneficial. The author recommends GIS as a tool for practical and efficient decision-making. It offers a set of capabilities in dealing with spatially referenced points, related data and information. In addition, it provides real time information that leads into making informed decisions (ibid). Implication is that an efficient and effective logistics system of unprocessed milk requires a better understanding of spatial distribution of milk collection centers in relation to both dairy farms and processing plants. This is possible with the aid of computer-based GIS systems. Similarly, in this study, farms and MBGs were spatially referenced features that were used as nodes in a road network to find shortest path(s) leading to enlightened decisions.

From a study conducted in Ireland about decision support tools in raw milk transportation, (O'Callaghan et al. 2021) report that milk collection schedules need to be dynamic as they are dependent on season of milk harvest. Bumper harvest translates to increased distance coverage and vice versa. This implies that there is variation of cost-distance as it either increases or decreases. Variables were collection schedules, season, tanker capacity and drivers. The researchers should have developed a model that would reduce travel distance regardless of whether milk is in or out of season. This research looks at milk delivery from the farm to the milk collection center aimed at reducing cost-distance irrespective of milk production.

Furthermore, a study in Sweden by (Bosona et al. 2013) investigated the need to integrate local food producers into the supply chain network in order to revamp competitiveness. GIS-based analysis was employed to come up with findings. Conclusions show advances in route optimization by reducing the number of routes, stops, transit time and travel distance. This study intends to simulate real-world routes into a GIS environment that is envisaged to reduce travel time based on distances from farm to MBG.

Development of dairy farmers in developing countries is sensitive to milk transportation strategies. Many smallholders are isolated and live far from processors. Poor roads, storage facilities, intermittent electricity supply, and long distances hamper logistical activities. These drawbacks result in traversing longer times before milk (highly perishable) is delivered to the processing machine.

A study investigated in Mongolia by Enkhtuya and Shin (2019) reveals that GIS mathematical optimization model reduces travel distance in the milk distribution network. This is achieved by finding better routes in a road network through GIS. Route optimization is attained by mapping farms, MBGs and roads in this context. This helped farmers to easily appreciate shortening of travel time in relation to travel distance since maps in GIS offer graphical reports that are easy to understand.

From Indonesia, Sahroni et al. (2018) report that they employed Open Source Spreadsheet Solver to generate optimal routes thereby minimizing traverse distance in transporting fast-moving consumer goods. Similarly, Using ArcMap, quickest routes between farms and MBGs were generated hence shortening traverse distances between two or more point features. This was achieved by using the Route tool from GIS Network Analyst.

In finding strategies to have a smooth transportation of unprocessed milk to the processor by Fussi (2010) in Tanzania, the investigator uncovered one milk collection center that closed due to disproportionality between high running costs of the center and low milk collection. The author argues that closing the facility was necessary due to poor business returns. Furthermore, farmers were advised to sell milk through informal markets. The study area had tarmac roads and electricity connections. From the list of findings and recommendations, GIS as a tool in transportation solver is excluded that might have solidified the researcher's claims. GIS based transportation system schedules routes using *Vehicle Routing Problem* extension that guides how to optimize assignment of vehicles based on capacity and sequence visits to milk collection centers.

In Uganda, Otaala (2016) debates that ICT brings efficiencies in agricultural value chains, precisely in dairy farming. The author argues that technology applications improve coordination between the smallholder dairy farmer and the purchaser. Furthermore, Otaala reveals that the dairy industry has a lot of information although its connection to prevention of milk deterioration is missing. Otaala needed to spend more time on the relationship between the dairy industry being "*intensive information*" and preservation of milk quality that is key in the value chain. The present study focused on efficiencies that a GIS-based transportation system contributed between the farm and MBGs to minimize traverse time and travel distance. This led to reducing further milk deterioration.

Rajeev et al. (2015) argue that information flow in dairy farming lags behind in relation to other agriculture sub sectors. Developing countries have acquired technologies from the developed countries. The challenge, however, is that most of the developing countries do not have the right infrastructure for the transfer of technology. They have limited resources, poor government policies, inadequate technology training centers, poor technology protection and negative attitudes towards technology. Developing countries are characterized by slow uptake of technology and the argument whether these technologies contribute significantly to alleviation of poverty or have positive socio-economic impact is still on going. This study introduced GIS technology in dairy industry so that farmers deliver milk in a timely and efficient manner resulting in positive payoffs.

In both developed and developing countries, previous studies on dairy sub-sector have tended to focus on socio-economic aspects of livestock development and vehicle routing problem. Particularly, from the milk collection centers to the processing plant with little evidence of studies between the farm and MBG in milk value chain. Therefore, this study focuses on simulating a milk transport system in a GIS environment using routes, farms and MBGs from the study area. Thereafter, spatial analyzes the transport system so that its impact to smallholder dairy farmers is beneficial.

In Malawi, a developing country where this study was conducted, there is little evidence that GIS technology exists in the milk supply chain. With the absence of GIS technology, transportation systems are fractured as quality of unprocessed milk is compromised by unsophisticated route schedules. Expectations were that GIS technology maps geographical locations for smallholder farms, MBGs and road network. Furthermore, a design of transport model that calculated metrics between incidents and facilities to support decision making by all agents in the value chain.

2.3 Spatial Analysis and Modelling

Of late, spatial data is in large volumes and readily available for use (Brunsdon and Comber, 2015). Tools like *R*, *GIS* among others are used to model mathematical systems, design graphical representations and analyze spatial data. The spatial data is used to model, visualize and analyze features in order to understand fundamental relationships and processes. However, Lin et, al 2018 argues that geospatial data is associated with some challenges like containing errors and large volume of data that makes it difficult to manage and analyze. These concerns need to be addressed before using them in GIS.

Contextually, the study adopts GIS from which Spatial Autocorrelation measured whether farms and MBGs as point features are random, uniform or clustered. Once patterns were identified on the map then the buffer tool assessed the radius between farms and MBGs. This was to determine if farms were located within the recommended 8 km radius or otherwise. In addition, *Network Analysis* tools; *route* and *Closest Facility* were engaged to analyze the model. The prototype connected farms and MBGs using a road network to determine traverse distances between point features. Eventually, this led to estimation of travel time using a route tool while Closest facility tool determined the nearest MBG(s) from the farm.

2.3.1 Spatial Autocorrelation

ArcMap has spatial statistical tools for analyzing distribution patterns. These tools constitute Average Nearest Neighbor, Getis-Ord General G, Incremental Spatial Autocorrelation, Ripleys K Function and Spatial Autocorrelation. Getis (2008) describes Spatial Autocorrelation as a concept that shows relationships between or among variables across georeferenced space. For example, given a set N in spatial units, Spatial Autocorrelation refers to association between some variable observed in every *n* localities and measure of geographical contiguity defined for all $n(n-1)$ pairs chosen from *n*. This means selection of the relationships and proximity between or among coordinated-farms and coordinated-MBGs in each of the cells in Thyolo district. According to Odland (2020), the aggregate of all spatial weights, denoted S, is defined by using

$$S = (N/W)*\Sigma\Sigma w_{ij}(x_i - \bar{x})(x_j - \bar{x})/\Sigma(x_i - \bar{x})^2 \tag{2.1}$$

Where N is the total number of features indexed between i and j while x is a variable of interest, $\bar{x}$ is the mean of x, w_{ij} is a matrix of spatial weights with zeroes on the diagonal i and j, W is the sum of w_{ij}.

The mathematical function shows the underlying geometrical structures of farms and MBGs in terms of patterns and correlations. Features (farms and MBGs) are represented by points with related attribute data on the map. The pattern of distribution of points can be random, uniform or clustered (Mansour, 2016; Floch et al. 2018) as shown in Figure 2.1. Flowerdew and Stillwell (2004), Illian et al. (2008) and Mansour (2016) have used the words random/dispersed, uniform/regular, cluster/aggregate interchangeably. Despite the use of different terminologies, the semantics is the same.

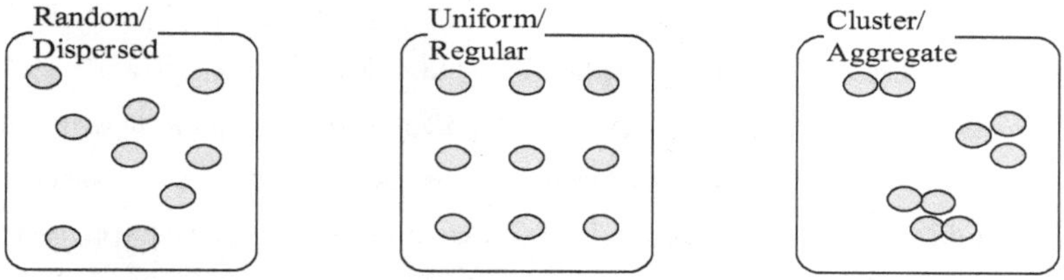

Figure 2.1: Three patterns of spatial distribution (Mansour, 2016)

After establishment of spatial patterns of farms and MBGs, GIS model measures Euclidean distances between point feature classes by using proximity analysis methods. The study employs a buffer tool. The tool is inbuilt in the GIS environment hence making it handy.

2.3.2 Buffer

Flowerdew and Stillwell (2004) affirm that buffer and overlay techniques are most used methods in identifying sites based on Euclidean distance. Similarly, Fazal (2008) argues that among the most important tools for testing spatial relationships between geometric structures is *buffer tool*. Buffer is a proximity function that creates a zone of specified distance around a selected point or polyline or polygon in a layer (Ahmed et al. 2018). This implies that buffer calculations of distances between two points occur in Cartesian space. For example, when coordinates of two points *a (a1, b1)* and *b (a2, b2)* are known in a Cartesian plane, then shortest traverse distance is determined using Pythagoras theorem. The shortest distance, d, between points a and b is given by

$$d = \sqrt{(\mathrm{a2} - \mathrm{a1})^2 + (\mathrm{b2} - \mathrm{b1})^2} \tag{2.2}$$

Therefore, the buffer tool uses the concept of Pythagoras theorem to calculate distances between points in a straight line. Once mapping of farms and MBGs was completed in GIS, then distances between them were calculated to determine 8 km radius or otherwise.

Kennedy and Kopp (2000) concludes that the Projected Coordinate System (PCS) is engaged when every point is identified by latitude and longitude on earth's surface around a localized region in a study area. PCS are preferred map projections in a local region as they are identified by latitudes and longitudes in a grid besides minimizing visual distortion of maps (Mulcahy and Clarke, 2001). Contextually, travel distances between farms and MBGs are measured on assumption that surface area of Thyolo is flat.

2.4 Network Analysis

Bolstad (2016) defines network analysis as a model of interconnected features that includes nodes and edges used to represent and analyze cost, distance and time. It helps in selecting the shortest route between point locations (Rai et al. 2005). There are *geometric networks* such as electricity, sewer, water that flows on edges in a single direction at a time and *network dataset* like roads, pedestrian, railway, airways that allow the agent to decide bidirectional traverse and destination (Bolstad, 2016). Modeling travel paths of a network provide analysis related to movement in that particular network (Thill, 2009; Alam, 2012).

Similarly, network analyst is a tool within GIS that solves common network problems such as finding optimal route, finding closest facility, identifying a service area, original-destination cost matrix, location allocation and vehicle routing problem on the network. It uses the principle of Dijkstra's Algorithm that solves routing problems based on variables such as time and distance (Nagrale et al. 2018). Sanjeevi and Shahabudeen (2015) enlightens that Dijkstra's Algorithm finds shortest route between source nodes via other nodes to destination nodes in a network while considering weight of edges as in Figure 2.2.

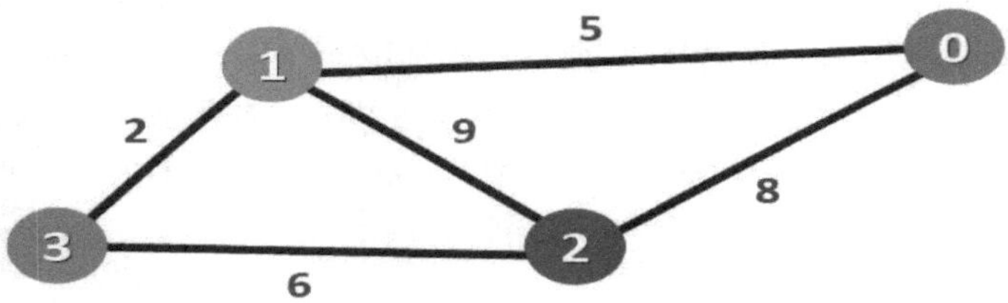

Figure 2.2: Dijkstra's Algorithm

Key

Node 0 = farm; Nodes 1, 2, 3 = MBGs; Black lines = edges; Digits = weight of edges

In finding the shortest route to deliver milk from the farm labelled 0 (grey node) to candidate MBGs labelled 1-3 (green, orange & purple nodes), the algorithm has to find the quickest travel route, determine nearest MBG and generate traverse directions. It should be highlighted that the algorithm only works with positive weights.

Therefore, this study models nodes (farms and MBGs) and edges (road network) in Thyolo and analyses the features using *route* and *Closest Analyst* network analyst extensions. Between nodes are edges represented as weight in form of distance and/or time. *Route* selects optimal path for a farmer to get to nearest MBG in the quickest time possible in relation to shortest distance.

2.4.1 Route

Route is a routing solver within Network Analyst in ArcMap environment based on Dijkstra's algorithm. It finds the shortest route by factoring in starting point to ending point following a sequence of rules (Da-bing and Jian-chuan, 2010). Likewise, the route consists of a one-way trip from the source (farm) to the destination (MBG) of unprocessed milk. In this study, the route starts at the farm and ends at the MBG. Rules are where to turn on junctions, path to follow and closest possible MBGs to deliver milk from a set of options. Related studies focused on Vehicle Routing Problem (VRP) where vehicles were involved in picking and delivery of milk between depots (Montoya-Torres et al. 2015; Braekers et al. 2016) excluding farmers who are crucial in the milk supply chain. Therefore, the milk transportation problem can only be complete if smallholder dairy farmers and any type of roads involved are incorporated.

Atkins (2017) highlights that there is direct and substantial impact between transportation and social and economic growth in rural Malawi. However, rural transportation is planned in a disintegrated way coupled with a non-holistic approach (ibid). Poor roads reduce mobility speed (Lall et al. 2009). Thyolo district is classified as a rural district in Malawi. According to Price et al. (2018), the country is predominantly rural based with an estimation of 84 % of the total population living in rural areas.

In Malawi, the classified road network is equal to 15451 km in length (Atkins, 2017). Lall et al. (2009) reports that main, secondary, tertiary, district and others are classes of roads. Villages that make rural areas connect to the classified roads using unclassified feeder paths. Transportation is concerned with speed that has factors of *distance* and *time*. Speed is the amount of distance travelled divided by time taken. Anecdotally, speed on the roads varies due to volume of traffic, roughness of the road, elevation of the terrain, direction of wind blowing, age-group, torque (for bicycle/motorcycle/car) among others irrespective of mode of transport. In Malawi, speeds in existence are those for classified roads and little evidence on unclassified paths.

2.4.2 Closest Facility

The layer measures the impedance between the incident and the facility; and identifies which facilities are nearest from the incident (Kharel and Shivananda, 2018). Incidents are origins while facilities are destinations. This infers that farms are incidents as milk transportation begins from there while MBGs are facilities since they are milk destinations. Closest facility determines the nearest facility from the incident. According to Charikar et al. (2001), this is guided by the following equation

$$r(C) \leq 2 *OPT \qquad (2.3)$$

Where r is the radius, C is the cost, 2 is approximated number of solutions and OPT are the Options

To find the nearest facility, the algorithm selects the first center C at random. Then selects the next center at random again whose length from C is greater than 2 by r. The process is repeated for all facilities using all vertices in the data set until all costs are calculated. Subsequently, the least distance is selected as nearest facility from the incident. Therefore, contextually, the equation selects the middle point of the farm. Then it chooses the next center for MBG whose distance is greater than 2 by following a set containing all vertices. Distances are calculated and compared where the shortest length between farm and MBG is selected hence closest milk facility.

2.5 Theoretical Framework

Grant and Osanloo (2014) define theoretical framework as an outline of the whole research that provides guidance on which to build and support a study. It serves as a fulcrum to research problem statement, objectives, significance and research questions within the study. More so, it provides specialized lens through which to examine data, conduct data analysis, interpret findings, address discoveries; and make recommendations and conclusions (Kivunja, 2018). The definition concludes that the theoretical framework is a blueprint of the whole study (Lim et al. 2009; Grant and Osanloo, 2014).

2.5.1 Decision Theory

Literature reports that Blaise Pascal and Pierre de Fermat invented Decision Theory in the 17th Century (Pascal & Fermat, 1654). Today, the theory is applied in various disciplines such as Mathematics, Politics, Actuarial Science, Philosophy, Psychology, Biology, Business, Social Science, and Statistics, among others (Parmigiani & Inoue, 2009).

Therefore, Decision Theory underpins this study. A theory concerned with determining best selection from possible available options where consequences are certainly unpredictable. Furthermore, this is an information systems research as it is concerned with routes optimization between incidents and facilities as the main objective. Therefore, a transport model was developed to address some milk delivery challenges. Information system research involves designing a system that solves a problem (Lim et al. 2009).

Hansson (2005) describes Decision Theory as a theory concerned with determining best selection from possible available options where consequences are certainly unpredictable. The author asserts that every situation has a problem that requires decision making by selecting optimal solutions from a pool of solutions. The theory is subdivided into normative (how decision should be made) and prescriptive decision (how decisions are actually made). The theory allowed farmers to choose shortest route to the MBG(s) hence decision-making. This helped to solve milk transportation problems from social economic point of view through four Decision Theory constructs namely Acts, Events, Outcomes and Payoffs.

(1) **Acts:** are actions being considered by the agent. In this scenario, the agent is the farmer. The action is the farmer delivering milk from farm to MBG using any mode of transport (foot, bicycle or motorcycle). From the set of choices on mode of transport, it is the farmer's discretion to deliver milk on foot, by bicycle or by motorcycle.

(2) **Events:** are occurrences taking place beyond the dairy farmer's control. For instance, if the farmer is delivering milk and finds that the bridge is washed away or the road is cut off due to floods, the farmer has to wait for construction of a makeshift bridge or road to proceed with the trip or look for alternative route that is passable. Shipping of milk is delayed that leads into longer travel time and milk deterioration. The farmer has no control over this eventuality.

(3) **Outcomes:** Are results of occurrences from acts and events. Results on acts would be variation of transit time to deliver milk due to variation of mode of transport chosen while result on events would be delay or complete failure in transporting milk to MBG due to poor state of the road.

(4) **Payoffs**: are values the decision maker places on occurrences. This could be positive or negative values. For example, positive payoff would be revenue realized after successfully delivering quality unprocessed milk to MBG while negative payoff would be failure to deliver milk to the MBG resulting in loss of income.

Just like any other theory, the theory constitutes variables that are either dependent or independent usually defined before the study (Babbie, 2013). Therefore, in this study, independent variables are mode of transport and distance travelled while dependent variable is travel time. Diagrammatically, the variables for this study are represented in the decision tree as shown in Figure 2.3.

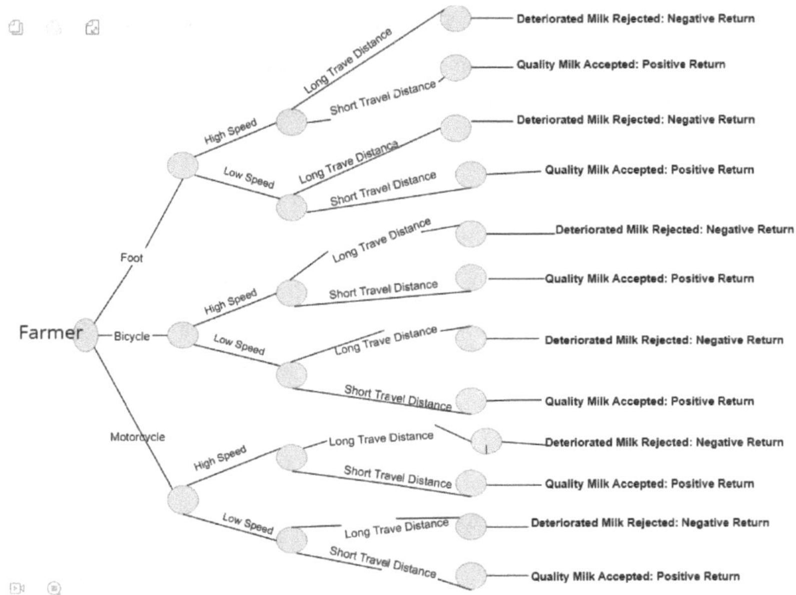

Figure 2.3: Decision Tree showing independent and dependent variables

Using Figure 2.3, GIS transport model assisted the farmer to select the best route based on least travel time from available options so that milk is delivered to the MBG as quickly as possible for chilling and storage. The selection helped the smallholder to prevent milk from being rejected at MBG due to deterioration. Consequently, the milk farmer realized a positive return from the milk supply.

It is envisaged that the Acts and the likely Events that Agents are subjected to such as road cut-offs due to floods, continuous heavy rainfall, and failure by MBGs to receive milk due to intermittent power supply affect farmer's income negatively (Sindani, 2012; Wiggins and Revoredo-Giha, 2016). Such eventualities require farmers to search for substitute facility that is second closest in order to deliver milk without compromising on quality. The longer it takes to deliver milk, the more the milk deteriorates. This negative Outcome leads to revenue losses. Avoiding milk losses is a positive Outcome that leads to stable economic gains among farmers as Payoff. This study came up with recommendations on integrating GIS into milk farming and how it could mitigate transportation challenges to smallholder dairy farmers in rural areas.

CHAPTER 3: METHODOLOGY

This chapter describes how the study was carried out to meet aims and objectives understudy. It discusses research strategy, study location, sample size and sampling, data collection, data analysis and ethical considerations.

3.1 Research Strategy

Creswell (2014) highlights that research approaches are strategies and processes that span decisions from broad paradigms to detailed methods of data collection, analysis and interpretation. This means a research approach is a focal point of philosophical postulations and methods in any study. Generally, research approaches are categorized into three classes, qualitative, quantitative and mixed methods (Creswell and Clark, 2018). Conventionally, qualitative research has its origins in social science, concerned with using non-numeric data with focus on understanding why things are the way they are in the social world and why people behave the way they do Babbie (2013). On the other hand, quantitative research is associated with natural sciences and deals with numeric data leading into addressing expressions such as how much, how many and how often. The author adds that numerical data has an edge over words as numbers measure some quality also.

The study that involves the use of a mixed approach is more powerful than either adoption of qualitative or quantitative research separately (Creswell and Clark, 2018). It provides detailed insights, integrates and synergizes on both qualitative and quantitative data (Dawadi et al. 2021). This implies that the strength of one research approach mitigates the weakness of another. Therefore, this study adopted both qualitative and quantitative approaches. Qualitative method was selected in order to determine challenges that dairy farmers face when transporting unprocessed milk to milk facilities. Conversely, the quantitative method was chosen because of calculations of travel time and travel distances. Using the GIS model to solve transport problems, numeric information was generated that showed distances from farms to MBGs and approximated milk delivery time in relation to transportation mode (foot, bicycle or motorcycle).

Silverman (2017) and Budai (2020) affirm that deductive approach moves from pre-existing general theory to specific observations. Therefore, a deductive approach was employed since data collection was used to assess the propositions in relation to *Decision Theory*. The collected data helped to understand observations of farmers through empirical data. Subsequently, confirm or reject research question. Due to time constraint, the cross-sectional study was used as it was corresponding with the nature of research objectives and question. Besides, the study was time bound as characterized by academic studies.

Furthermore, research design is concerned with how data was collected, what instruments were employed and how data was analyzed (Zohrabi, 2013). There are several research designs that includes case study, ethnography and field experiment (Easterbrook et al. 2008; Creswell, 2014; Wohlin and Aurum, 2015). The researcher adopted field experiment in optimizing routes when transporting milk from farm to milk MBGs. Babbie (2013) defines field experiment as a method where observation and interpretation of a study subject is conducted in its natural setting. Data was collected through interviews, observation, published articles and questionnaire in smallholder farmer's natural environment, which was later interpreted. For field data collection, the researcher visited livestock experts at Blantyre Agricultural Development Division (BLADD), Thyolo District Animal Health and Livestock Development Officer (TDAHLDO), extension workers, Shire Highlands Milk Producers Association (SHMPA) and Farmers Milk Producers Association (FAMPA) executive members, dairy farmers and MBGs in their respective working setups.

3.2 Study Location

The study was carried out in Thyolo district, one of the 28 districts of Malawi. Administratively, Thyolo is located in the southern region of Malawi and lies on Shire Highlands plateau with elevation averaging 2, 000 – 4,000 feet. The plateau has cooler temperatures making it a conducive environment for dairy breeding, as cows are less susceptible to heat stress and diseases (Wiggins & Revoredo-Giha, 2016). The district covers an area of 1,666 km^2 with population density of 433.0/km^2 (NSO, 2018). Much of the land is covered with tea, coffee and macadamia estates. It has a population of 587 452 (Sustainable Rural Growth & Development Initiative Project, 2018) of which the percentage of dairy farmers is not clearly known. The district was purposely chosen because it is the highest milk production district in Malawi averaging 1.5 million liters per month (M-Livestock Consultant, 2016). Subsequently, milk sales translate to highest revenue earning for smallholders of this district as compared to other districts in the country. Therefore, it was important to understand how milk is transported presently and the pitfalls that farmers encounter. This assisted in tailoring an appropriate solution to solve milk transportation challenges.

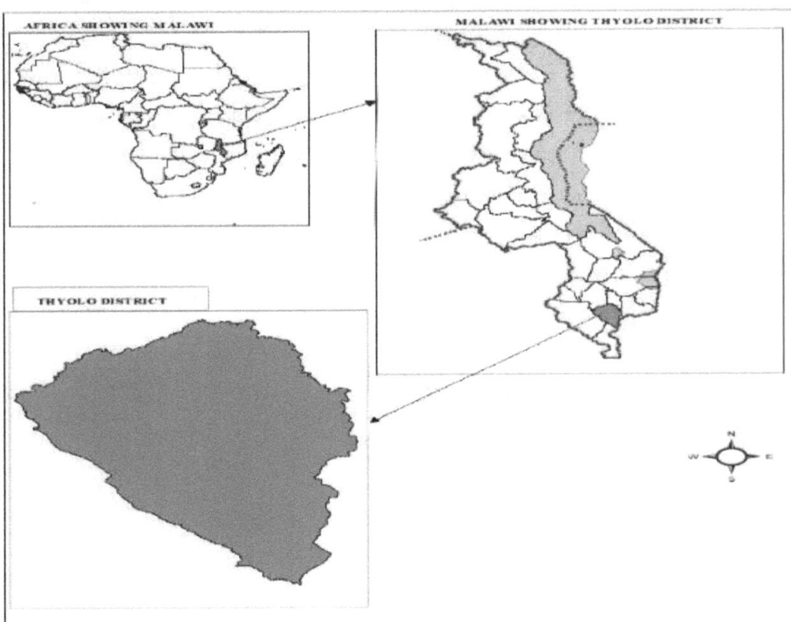

Figure 3.1: Maps of Africa, Malawi showing location of Thyolo district

3.3 Sampling

Babbie (2013) defines sampling as a procedure for selecting units of observations with the aim of generalizing from the sample to the population. Therefore, purposive sampling was used to collect in-depth data on this investigation from dairy farmers in their research setting. The research targeted respondents who were presumed influential, knowledgeable, experienced, available and willing to participate. The farmers and bulking groups in Thyolo district were considered as a population.

All 48 milk collection centers in the case study were involved because the research needed to capture coordinates for every MBG that would support creation of exact locations on Earth's surface in GIS. The study started by engaging the Milk Bulking Group leadership (Chairperson or Secretary or representative) who were deemed to be effective, conversant, experienced, accessible and willing to take part in data collection exercise.

Out of the total number of milk collection centers, only 4 (Goliati, Namahoya, Nakhwakwe and Okhalhavo) were purposively selected. The four milk groups were selected because they were closer to the researcher's residence as compared to other milk collection centers. The distance involved was about 35 kilometers so it was easier to navigate. Thereafter, 50 respondents from each of the four Milk Bulking Groups were targeted.

The study targeted 50 farmers from Namahoya Milk Bulking Group whose farms were physically visited in order to capture farm coordinates for production of maps. This would assist to create routes between farms and milk facilities. The routes would reveal time taken and distance covered, Subsequently, understand milk transportation challenges. Leadership from all four bulking groups selected farmers from the list of names contrary to the study's plan. Their reasoning was that the researcher might choose a farmer who might have changed Milk Bulking Groups or stopped dairy farming or whose farm cannot be traced. Therefore, selection of the sampled population might have been biased.

3.4 Data Collection

It particularly involved collecting data from published articles and documents. However, field data collection began on 22nd June 2020 and ended on 30th April 2021. Interviews, observations and questionnaires were used to collect primary data while published articles were engaged to source secondary data. All these tools were used to ensure proper triangulation of data and results.

Physically, all (48) but Mtambanyama MBGs in Thyolo were visited. Mtambanyama was left out due to limited travelling resources; however, geographical coordinates were captured using two different websites. These sites produced similar output. The visits were primarily to interview MBG officers and to capture geographical coordinates. Two MBGs (Mpeni and Nanjodi) were not yet open for operations as they were under construction but coordinates were also captured.

3.4.1 Interview

BLADD, SHMPA, FAMPA, TDAHLDO, MBG leaders and farmers were interviewed face-to-face with the objective of understanding how milk transportation from farm to MBG is done. Semi- structured interviews were used throughout the exercise. Interviewees were briefed on the purpose of the interviews to evade bias and recounting of other issues irrelevant to the topic under study.

Locating MBGs to interview leadership and capture coordinates was a challenge as locations and total number of MBGs were unclear. This was due to the fact that SHMPA provided an excel sheet that was last updated in 2017. It contained attribute fields namely: - MBG name, chairperson name and cell phone number. Due to the gap between the last update and the time contact details were collected, some numbers were unreachable, some contact persons were no longer leaders while others went through. TDAHLDO only provided the list of MBGs without contact names and cellphone numbers. This led to visitations of some MBGs without booking appointments. The researcher relied on getting directions to MBGs by asking passersby. The reason to have direct contacts in advance was to pre-inform the leadership about the study and pending visits.

Prior to field data collection, the researcher had several meetings with the academic supervisor. The motive was to prepare and get guidance on field data collection. On the first day, the supervisor accompanied the researcher to give on-site direction on pilot. At the end of the day, themes and interview guide were developed (see Appendix A). The themes road-mapped the researcher in subsequent solo interviews. Table 3.1 shows interviews that were conducted.

Table 3.1: Interviews Conducted

STAKEHOLDER	ORGANIZATION	INTERVIEWEES
Malawi Government	BLADD	1
Malawi Government	Thyolo DALDO	1
NGO	SHMPA	1
NGO	FAMPA	1
Leadership	MBGs in Thyolo	45
Farmers	Namahoya	50
TOTAL		**99**

While visiting the MBGs and farmers, coordinates of MBGs and farms were captured using a handheld Garmin GPS receiver shown in Figure 3.2. To record accurate coordinates of a location, the researcher held the device under clear sky where obstruction was non-existent. More so, coordinates were recorded at an accuracy +/-3 meters. The same coordinates were also manually recorded in a book to ensure a backup is available. Thereafter, recordings were transferred into Microsoft excel for further data Organization before saving in a comma-separated values format; ready to upload into GIS. Kariithi (2008) and Ngigi and Wangai (2012) used the same handheld device in studies related to this investigation.

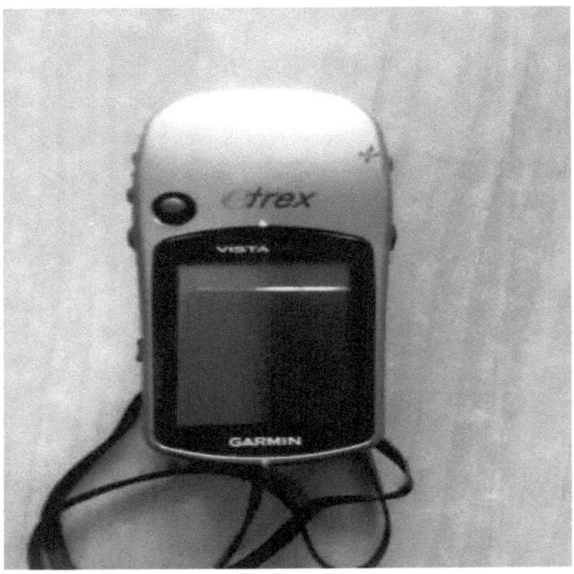

Figure 3.2: Handheld Garmin GPS receiver

3.4.2 Questionnaire

The study targeted 200 farmers from four different MBGs as tabulated in Table 3.2. The English version of the questionnaire (See Appendix B) was translated into Chichewa (Malawi's national language) version to ensure that there was no language barrier. The test items were aligned to the objectives of the study.

Table 3.2: MBGs against Target Population

MBG NAME	TARGET POPULATION
Goliati	50
Nakhwakwe	50
Namahoya	50
Okhalhavo	50
Total	**200**

Smallholder dairy farmers are already clustered in cooperatives known as Milk Bulking Groups. At every bulking group, the executive committee selected respondents from the list of names contrary to the study's plan. Their reasoning was that they were familiar with respondents that can reply objectively to the questions.

Design and categorization of the questionnaire was based on general dairy farmer's information, milk production, transportation and constraints. The design included both open-ended and closed-ended questions. The researcher pre-tested the questions with Bvumbwe Milk Bulking Group respondents to ensure questions were understandable. Flaws were noted. Subsequently, changes were made and the questionnaires were administered on Goliati, Nakhwakwe, Namahoya & Okhalhavo milk facilities.

Prior to administration of the questionnaire the consent note (see appendix C) was translated into the local language (Chichewa) to circumvent language barrier. It was read aloud in the midst of respondents to enlighten them of the study, expectations and their rights. Apart from the researcher, executives helped in the administration of questionnaires. In some instances, respondents were completing the questionnaires on their own. Figure 3.3 shows a meeting that was held at Okhalhavo MBG after completing the questionnaires.

Figure 3.3: Photo of a Meeting Held at Okhalhavo MBG

3.4.3 Observation

Observations are classified as participatory and non-participatory . Participatory observation is when the data collector is actively involved in activities being observed as opposed to non-participant where the researcher stays separate from activities being observed in order to understand a phenomenon in a society (Leavy, 2017). Therefore, the study adopted a non-participant option since the activities were observed passively by the investigator. The option was carried out for every field visitation to check whether data that was presented during interviews and questionnaires was close to or different from what was on the ground.

3.5 Geoprocessing

Garrard (2016) defines geoprocessing as a way of manipulating spatial data which is either in raster or vector format. In this study, the base map for Malawi and surrounding countries was collected from the Survey Department under the Ministry of Lands, scanned using a plotter Figure 3.4 and stored in a flash disk. The scanned images were kept in *jpeg* picture format that were later imported in ArcMap environment. The resultant files/layers were then georeferenced in order to relate features with the real world of *X* and *Y* coordinates. Thereafter, digitizing cadastral layers to produce international boundary, district boundary, district headquarters, rivers, road network, landuse, landcover and railway line. The layers were then superimposed together with farms and MBGs datasets. Shifts in point locations of farms and MBGs were noted as they were collected in World Geodetic System 1984 (WGS84) format by the researcher. This prompted re-projection of the layers to Malawi's local projection system of 1950 Universal Transverse Mercator 36 South (1950 UTM 36 South) so as to conform with approved cadastral maps from the department of survey.

Figure 3.4: Plotter scanning base map

At this point, it was imperative to create a geodatabase so that all layers were kept in one location for easy access and management. Allen and Coffey (2019) and Bajjali (2018) assert that it is important to store data in a geodatabase since it optimizes performance in terms of file sharing, compression and updating.

Then the 8 km as distance value was entered in the linear unit field to create a buffer polygon around the input feature, Namahoya. Alam (2012) asserts that calculation of buffer zones is based on Euclidean distance represented by the expression below.

$$(p, q) = \sum_{i=1}^{n} (q_i + p_i)^\wedge 2 \qquad (3.1)$$

where *p,q* is the length between 2 points in Euclidean space.

q1 and *p1* are vectors as original and destination respectively

n is number of spaces

More so, the database as target output feature class was selected to store the buffered polygon. Unit of measure (km) was selected from the drop down menu. In the Dissolve *field*, option *none* is selected to display the merging of 50 farms sharing Namahoya.

3.5.1 Building Network Dataset

In order to build the network dataset, *road network* and *landcover* layers were first stored in geodatabase before digitization. Digitizing of a feature is done by streaming, tracing or freehand (Bolstad, 2016). Contextually, freehand was adopted to digitize the roads from the satellite imagery to create a road network. The purpose of creating a road network was to connect farms and MBGs through roads. Figure 3.5 shows a road network in Thyolo district.

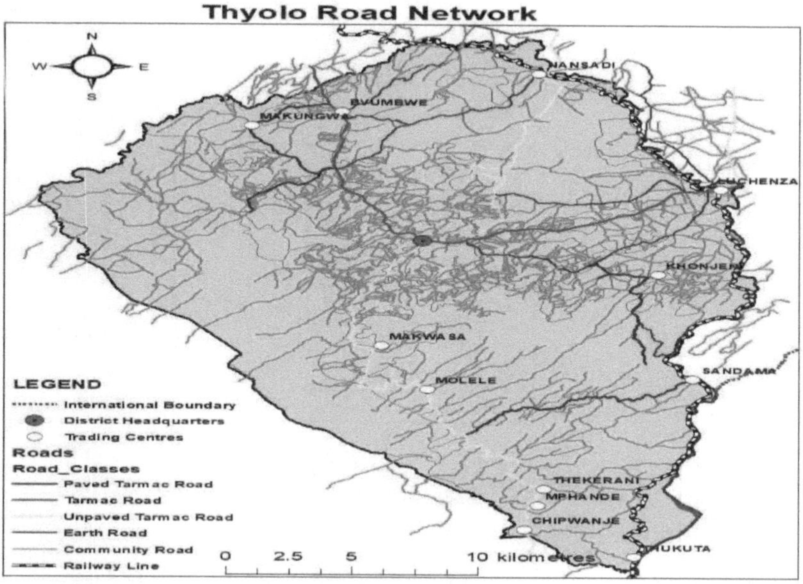

Figure 3.5: Road Network in Thyolo district

Three fields for *Time*, *Distance* and *Speed* were added in the attribute table of the road network. Units for time, distance and speed were set to hours, kilometers and kilometers/hour, respectively; and data type as integer in the road network data set. To calculate time and/or length, *time* and *speed* were set to use a field calculator while *distance* was configured to use a geometry calculator. Network dataset constituted nodes, edges and weights representing farms/ MBGs, roads and times/distances respectively that supported network analysis. More so, *Time* and *maximum speeds* for all 3 modes of transport were added as other attributes in the table of road shape file. Loll et al. (2009) and Dos Anjos Luis and Cabral (2016) argue that average speeds for footing, bicycling and motorcycling were 5 km/hour, 20 km/hour and 34 km/hour, respectively. Therefore, in this study, the same speeds were adopted.

Therefore, a transport model was designed using data collected from Thyolo district. Data included coordinates, road network, land usage and land coverage. This was attained by using geo-processing operators; spatial autocorrelation, buffer, route analysis and closest facility. Figure 3.6 shows a design of a transport model in a flow chart format

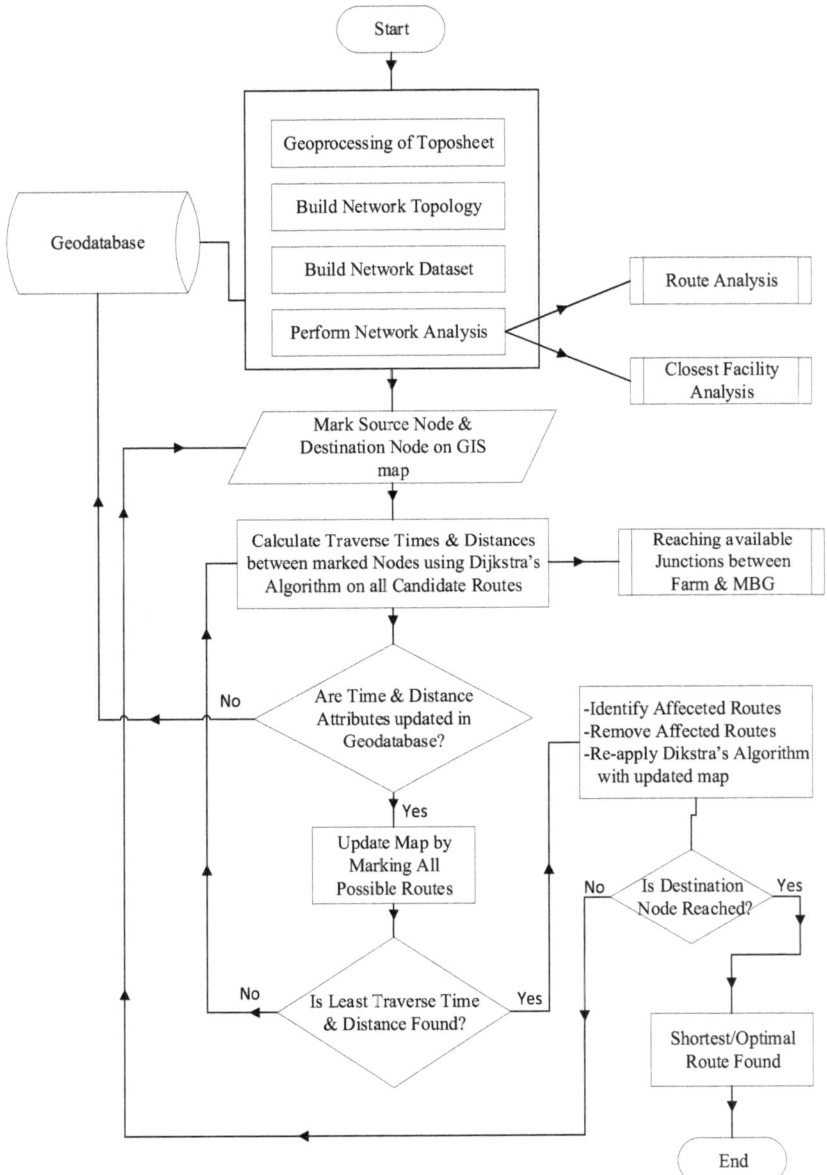

Figure 3.6: Transport Model Presented in Flow Chart

3.6 Document Analysis

Document analysis is a qualitative research technique used to examine documents in an Organization to give meanings and interpretations (Bowen, 2009). The documents include both electronic and physical ones. In this study, milk annual reports, guidelines to run daily operations at milk bulking groups, rules and regulations and milk supply records (see appendix D) were analyzed effectively in order to promote understanding and knowledge.

3.7 Data Analysis Techniques

Data analysis is the process of summarizing data collected by interpreting it through a systematic and analytical approach to determine patterns and relationships McKinney (2012); Ratner (2017). For this study, the collected data was used to build themes and categories in relation to activities of transporting unprocessed milk. The network analysis extensions (Route Analysis and Closest Facility Analysis) produced transit time and distance covered that was used to make meanings. Thereafter, a spatial analysis approach was used to analyze distribution patterns and relationships of farms, milk bulking groups and road network.

Spatial analysis is the application of one or more GIS operations to GIS data in order to solve real-world problems. The approach involves output of one operation that serves as input of the other operation. In this study, operators Spatial Autocorrelation and Buffer Analysis together with two network analysis extensions were used to solve the real transportation problem of milk delivery in Thyolo district, Malawi. Spatial Autocorrelation analyzed geographical distribution patterns of farms and MBGs. Buffer assessed the straight-line distance between farms and MBGs if they were located between the recommended radiuses of 8 km or not. Route Analysis assisted in finding shortest route based on time in relation to mode of transport while Closest Facility Analysis facilitated location of nearest MBGs from farms.

3.8 Validity and Reliability of Data

The researcher ensured direct phone lines were obtained during field visits. The motive was to make follow-up calls where notes were improperly recorded. Phone numbers were encrypted in a language that was understood by the researcher only. In addition, the phone was password-protected. Analysis and compilation of data collected was done in the evenings of the same day. This principle was observed throughout the exercise for easy recollection. The data collection methods included interviews, observation and questionnaire that focused on similar questions to mine data from all players involved in unprocessed milk transportation. This was just one way of triangulating data to solidify its validity, reliability and interpretation as alluded by (Zohrabi, 2013).

3.9 Ethical Consideration

It is necessary to seek consent from concerned authorities before commencement of data collection. One basis of conducting effective and meaningful research in studies is ethics such that the behavior and conduct are always under scrutiny in the setup of the research. It is necessary to consider ethics as they promote values such as truth, knowledge, collaborative work and error-free (Resnik, 2015). Furthermore, ethics ensures accountability to the public who supports the research (ibid).

The University of Malawi, through the Programme Coordinator of MSc in Informatics, drafted a reference letter (See Appendix E) in March 2020, which was photocopied and presented to all targeted institutions. This was to ascertain that indeed the researcher was a student at the University and sought to collect data from their institutions and members in their respective working environments.

Furthermore, the researcher scribed Blantyre Agricultural Development Division, Shire Highlands Milk Producers Association, Suncrest Cremaries Limited and Dairibord Malawi Limited (See Appendix F) seeking permission to carry out a research in their territories/institutions in which it was clearly indicated that the study would be purely for academic purposes. The institutions were selected because they are physically located in the southern region of Malawi where the area under study is located. All but Suncrest responded positively (See Appendices G, H & I).

The researcher sought verbal consent from the MBG executive committees and farmers as guided by SHMPA in the approval letter. The authorization to carry out the research was granted by the MBG executive committee. The researcher explained the purpose of the study to MBG committee members and assured the would-be respondents that information they provide shall be exclusively for academic purposes and that identities of respondents would be masked. Sensitive findings from the study would be dealt with in a manner not to destroy dairy farming. Field data collection started when all conditions were met satisfactorily.

CHAPTER 4: RESULTS AND DISCUSSIONS

This chapter presents and discusses research findings. Results are discussed in relation to study objectives and research question of this study. Farms, MBGS, roads, rivers, boundaries, land cover and land usage simulate real-world features as thematic maps in GIS. Therefore, the chapter has three broad headings of farms, Milk Bulking Groups and spatial modelling.

Contextually, spatial modelling constitutes Spatial Autocorrelation, Buffer Analysis, Route Analysis and Closest Facility Analysis. *Spatial Autocorrelation* identifies positions and distribution pattern(s) of farms and MBGs while *Buffer analysis* investigates whether every farm is discretely located within a recommended radius of 8 km or not from Namahoya milk facility. More so, *route analysis* selects the optimal route by finding shortest traverse times in relation to distances between point features in the catchment area. Closest facility analysis finds one or more milk facilities from the farm based on travel time.

4.1 Farm

The first objective of this study is to identify problems faced by smallholder farmers when transporting milk to MBGs. It was therefore paramount to understand the current distribution chain of unprocessed milk and related activities. The supply chain constitutes stakeholders such as dairy smallholder farmers, traders and consumers. Activities include milking, transportation to sell at MBG and collection through tankers by dairy companies for processing. The processed milk is later delivered to supermarkets where consumers purchase. Figure 4.1 shows present unprocessed milk supply chain particularly how distribution occurs from the farm to various destinations.

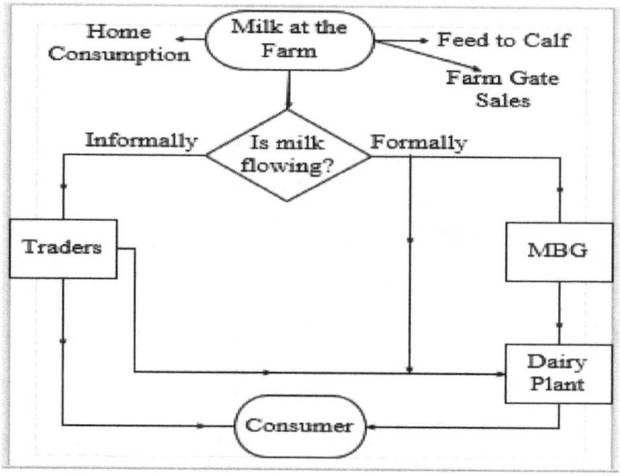

Figure 4.1: Informal and formal milk flow

The study finds that some milk is left for the calf, some taken for home consumption, some sold at the gate and some is sold to either traders or MBGs. Usually, traders buy milk at very low prices from dairy farmers. Consequently, they fetch more money by vending to consumers or processors directly. Anecdotal evidence shows that traders dictate the price. However, other farmers decide to supply milk straight to the processing plant. Informal milk flow involves selling of raw milk to traders or through farm-gates. Formal milk flow constitutes selling milk straight to the milk factory or bulking group.

Findings show that farmers transport milk in churns mainly on foot or bicycles to milk collection centers for bulk storage, chilling and subsequent collection by processors. This is a recommended channel by the Government of Malawi (C. Revoredo-Giha & Toma, 2016). Formal milk supply involves a dairy farmer delivering to sell milk at milk collection center where it is later picked by the processor using tankers. Milk is processed and packaged at the milk factory before delivered to various outlets for retailing or consumption. Figure 4.2 shows the current transportation system of unprocessed milk and associated activities from the farm via MBG to the processor.

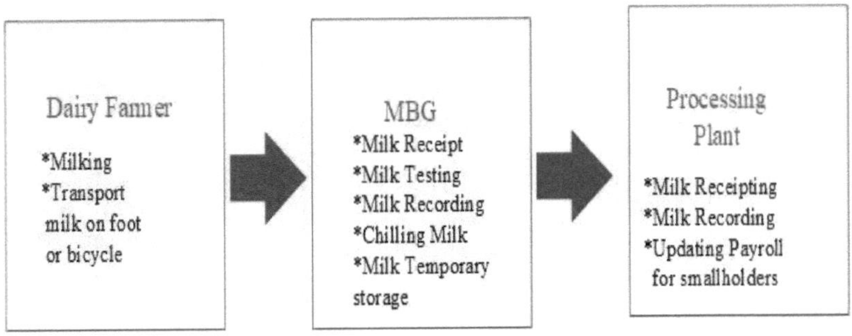

Figure 4.2: Milk flow and activities from farm to processor

Drawing from acts as construct, activities such as milking time, setout time and transport mode are decided by the farmer. It is entirely at the discretion of the farmer when, how, what, where to transport milk. Therefore, the agent considers when, where, what, why and how factors to ensure milk transported and accepted for sell at MBG. However, hiccups like unpassable road due to washed away bridge, road cut off are some of the drawbacks in the supply chain. Resultantly, farmers fail to deliver milk to the MBG. The outcome is that farmer's payoff is negatively affected as lamented by one respondent:

> *"I wish the government of Malawi built proper and strong roads for us since we contribute to the economy of the country in terms of food sufficiency and employment. On weekly basis during rainy season, I fail to deliver milk because of poor road network. During dry season, MBGs sometimes cannot buy our milk because of perpetual electricity outages. Milk needs cooling and the national grid powers our tanks. In the absence of electricity then farmers, suffer lost-sales, as there are no milk market options."*

4.1.1 Mode of Transport

Interrogation on most used mode of transport was done on 50 farmers of Namahoya when delivering milk to the facility. Mode of transport was grouped into foot, bicycle, motorcycle, vehicle and wheelbarrow. The question on mode of transport emphasized on most frequent means of milk transportation despite availability of other options for some farmers. Findings show that farmers transport milk to the MBG either on foot or by bicycle or by motorcycle Figure 4.3. Alternation of the three modes of transport was also observed. For example, on certain days, delivery of milk is on foot while on other days is by bicycle. In most cases, this happens when the bicycle is dysfunctional. Figure 4.3 shows number of farmers against mode of transport.

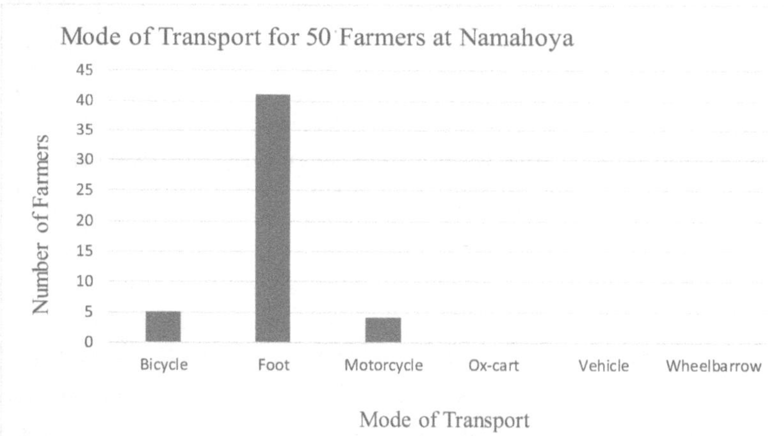

Figure 4.3: Number of Farmers Against Mode of Milk Transportation.

Figure 4.3 shows that out of 50 farmers, 5 use bicycles when transporting milk, representing 10% while 41 travel on foot representing 81%. Only 4 use motorcycles representing 8 % and no one transports milk by ox-cart nor vehicle nor wheelbarrow. Results indicate that walking is the most used mode of transport. The result is in agreement with findings by Palk et al. (2020).

Results from interviews also reveal that even those that bicycled and motorcycled frequently walked (95%) when delivering milk to Namahoya due to perpetual breakdowns of the cycles. This revelation is in agreement with findings by Raballand et al. (2011) that walking was the commonest mode of transport in rural areas of Sub-Saharan African countries including Malawi where this study occurred. Therefore, walking when transporting milk to bulking groups requires information on travel time and travel distance. Ultimately, this information supported farmers to schedule trips effectively leading to reduced milk deterioration and subsequent acceptance of milk at bulking groups.

The study observed that there is a railway line that runs through southern part of Thyolo even though it was excluded as mode of transport in the interviews and questionnaire. Furthermore, the railway line was under maintenance and no train was running its operations at the time of this investigation. Besides, when the train is servicing the route, it has a weekly schedule making it difficult for farmers to rely on it since milk delivery occurs once or twice daily. Therefore, the exclusion of railway line as mode of travel did not affect the results in any way.

4.2 MBG

Administratively, Thyolo comprises seven TAs and four Senior Chiefs. Recently, TA Chimaliro was further subdivided into Boidi and Nanseta TAs and falls under jurisdiction of Paramount Chief Ngolongoliwa. MBG officials that surround the Ngolongoliwa headquarters did not differentiate between Paramount Chief and TA. They cited Paramount Chief Ngolongoliwa as their 'TA' when the Chief is at a higher level, superintending a group of TAs.

4.2.1 Grouping of MBGs by TA

The real-world ofTAs is modelled in ArcMap. Consequently, the thematic map of TAs together with member MBGs is prototyped. The map displayed distribution pattern of milk facilities as point locations and TAs as polygons. Findings indicate that MBGs are more aggregated in TAs Chimaliro and Bvumbwe than other remaining 4 TAs. On the contrary, they are non-existent in TAs Changata, Kapichi, Nsabwe, Thukuta and SC Mbawela. This is due to variation in landcover. Erection of MBGs depends on pasture for cows. On the other hand, milk facilities exist in fewer numbers or not at all because the terrain exist on a plateau and pasture exist in minimal quantities. This means that the occurrence of the MBG as a point feature on Earth's surface has equal probability while independent of one another. Point feature MBG is more concentrated in the North, North East and North West of Thyolo than in other cardinal and ordinal points.

Statistics of Milk Bulking Groups under Traditional Authorities is displayed in Figure 4.4.

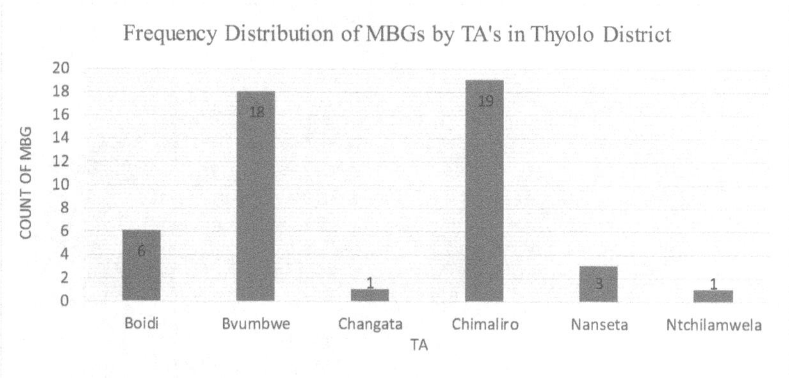

Figure 4.4: Frequency Distribution of MBGs by TA's in Thyolo District

The graph shows the frequency of MBGs by TA's in Thyolo district. Total number of MBGs was 48. TA Chimaliro has the highest number of bulking groups, totaling 19, representing 39.5%. TA Bvumbwe has 18 MBGs that translates to 37.5%. TAs Boidi and Nanseta comprise 6 and 3 MBGs representing 12.5% and 6.25% respectively. TA Ntchilamwela and SC Kwethemule consist of a single MBG each representing a combined percentage of 4.16%. Variation of number of MBGs was dependent of availability of pasture suitable for cows. Areas for TA's Chimarilo and Bvumbwe are located in the north and north-east of Thyolo district where grass as feed for cow is in abundance. Other TA's lie on high elevation where land usage cannot be translated into grazing.

4.2.2 MBG-Processor Analysis

ArcMap shows grouping of MBGs based on processors. Every MBG subscribes to a single processor at any given time. Figure 4.5 shows categorization and spatial distribution of MBGs against processors.

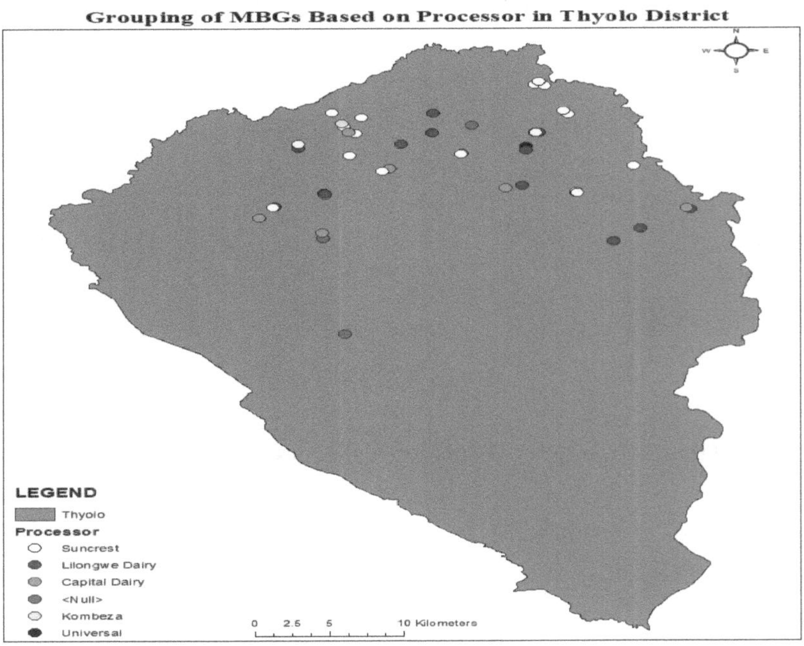

Figure 4.5 Categorization and Distribution of MBGs based on processor

Results in Figure 4.5 show that MBGs are aligned to 5 processors. Processors are Suncrest, Lilongwe Dairy, Capital Dairy, Kombeza and Universal. Suncrest has the highest milk collection share of 21 MBGs representing 47 % followed by Lilongwe Dairy with 15 representing 33%. Capital Dairy collects milk from 7 MBGs representing 16 % while Kombeza and Universal collects from 1 MBG each representing 2% each. During field data collection, 2 MBGs (Mpeni & Nanjodi) were under construction while 1 (Mtambanyama) was snubbed because it is an outlier. This means that neither the executive members nor farmers were interviewed to find out problems that they face when transporting milk. Consequently, it is difficult to attach these 3 MBGs to any processor.

4.2.3 MBG-Association Analysis

Some MBGs belong to an Association as discussed in chapter 2. These associations are SHMPA and FAMPA while others subscribe to none. Therefore, MBGs are further categorized based on association. Figure 4.6 shows cartographic distribution and one-to-one relationship between MBG and association.

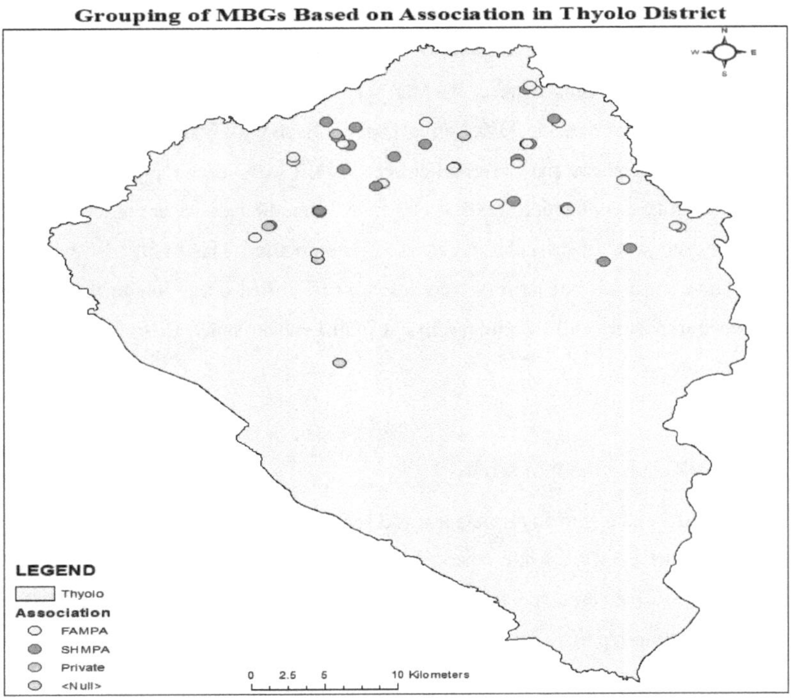

Figure 4.6 Distribution Pattern and 1-to-1 Relationship between MBG and Association

Findings in Figure 4.6 shows that FAMPA has 22 (48.89%) while SHMPA has 20 (44.44%). The remaining 3 (6.67%) labelled "*private*" do not pertain to any association. Considering distribution patterns based on association helped in identifying factors that lead in selecting them over other ones.

4.2.4 Farm-MBG Analysis

Fifty farms that transport and sell milk to Namahoya together with a few MBGs that surround it in the observation window were sampled. The map showed dairy farms whose farmers deliver milk to Namahoya despite being in proximity to other MBGs. This means that some farmers bypass nearby MBGs and travel longer distances to

Namahoya. In tandem to this revelation, is data collected through interviews. When asked why some farmers bypass nearest MBGs and deliver milk to Namahoya? For example, some interviewees pointed out that:

"Choice of MBG is based on reasons such as "good" leadership at the MBG, timely receipt of monthly sales revenue, good pricing per liter since processors buy milk at different prices per liter, access to loans in form of cows, cow feeds and cow pass-on program. "

Cow pass-on program is giving a dairy cow to a farmer where first beneficiary gives the first-born female calf to another farmer. Smallholder dairy farmers prefer MBGs which has cow pass-on scheme. The finding concurs with that of Thomson et al. (2020).

In addition, some responded that;

> "*There are other loan facilities like farm inputs such as fertilizers and pesticides that are accessed by farmers since we take into account their monthly revenue. That acts as surety".*

On the other hand, another participant mentioned that same reasons as that of Namahoya chairperson. However, the respondent added that:

> "*The facility runs a Savings and Credit Cooperative that offers cash savings and credit services to farmers that are members of the MBG. So that's why farmers subscribe to particular MBGs as others do not have such programs."*

4.3 Spatial Modelling

Under this section, spatial modelling discussed *spatial autocorrelation* that analyzed distribution patterns of 50 sampled farms that subscribe to Namahoya MBG and all 48 MBGs. In addition, *a buffer tool* determined whether the 50 farms were located within or outside the recommended 8 km radius from Namahoya. *Route Analysis* calculated traverse time and travel distance based on mode of transport (foot, bicycle and motorcycle) while the *closest facility analysis* identified the nearest MBG (s) from the farm.

4.3.1 Spatial Autocorrelation

The second objective of this study is to assess spatial distribution of farms and MBGs in Thyolo district. To achieve that, it was imperative to engage spatial autocorrelation in GIS. Spatial autocorrelation analyses distribution patterns of point locations (farms & MBGs) in the study area. The technique provides a very useful spatial statistical model in analyzing observed patterns of points where points represent locations in a bounded region. Points represent the location of farms and MBGs in Thyolo.

At this point, there is need to scientifically determine whether the distribution pattern is random, uniform or clustered. Therefore, running spatial correlation in ArcMap generates the spatial autocorrelation report shown in Figure 4.7

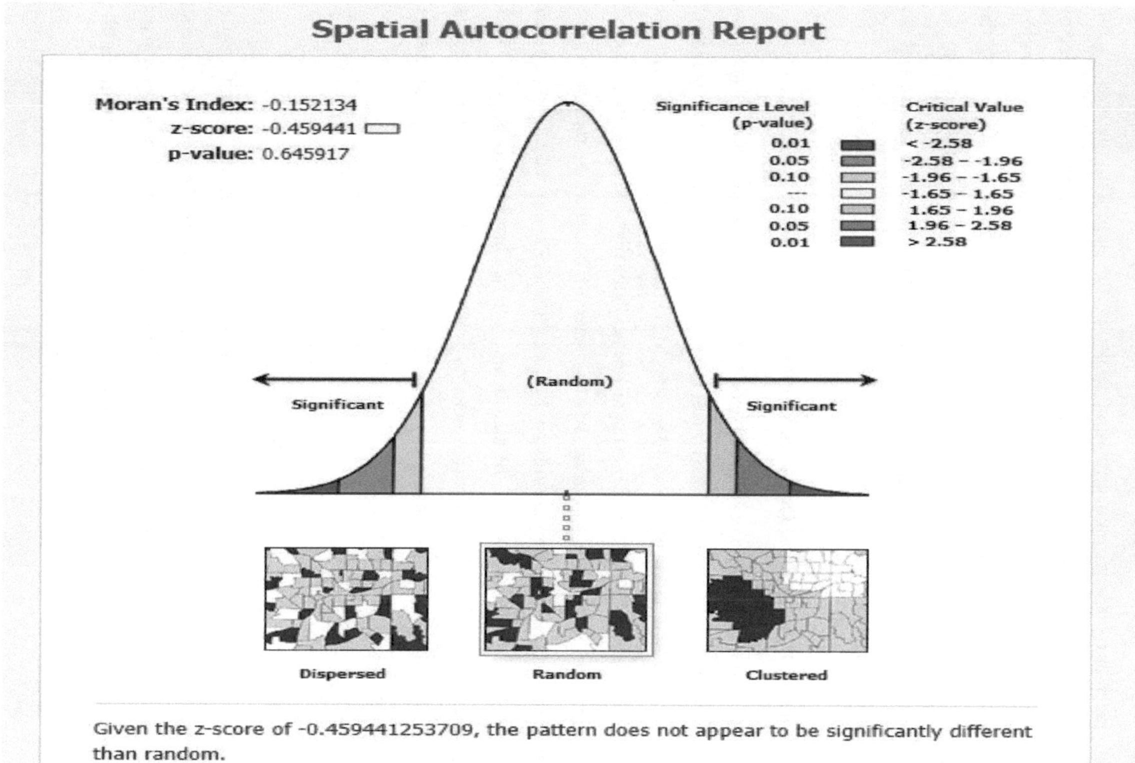

Figure 4.7: Spatial Autocorrelation Report

Neighborhood search threshold is 10107.2388 meters. This means that when calculating spatial autocorrelation statistics, the algorithm determines the size of the area and makes a decision for each MBG as a point feature. The value of Moran's index is a negative number, -0.152134 that shows that there is a distribution of distinct values near each MBG. The z-score is -0.459441 meaning that the MBGs are randomly distributed while the p-value is 0.645917 indicating that the value is not statistically significant. High values and Low values in the dataset are possible results of random spatial processes.

(a) Calculate Distance Band from Neighborhood

Calculate Distance Band from Neighborhood tool identifies the minimum, maximum and average distance where any MBG as an input parameter has at least one neighbor from a set of MBGs. Running the tool by using MBG dataset calculates minimum one neighbor distance of 13.92 meters, maximum one neighbor distance as 10106.23 meters & average one neighbor distance of 959.66 meters. The value of maximum one neighbor distance is in agreement with the distance threshold computed through *Spatial Autocorrelation* tool that analyzed the distribution pattern. Distance between one MBG to the next is averaging 960 meters (corrected to 1 significant number) and the value is used in *Incremental Spatial Autocorrelation* tool as beginning distance to further analyze the distribution pattern.

(b) Incremental Spatial Autocorrelation

To identify the extent to which distance of MBGs is maximized through spatial autocorrelation clustering phenomenon, distribution patterns happen at diverse scales; therefore, it is essential to find the distance at which clustering is most pronounced. Running the *incremental spatial autocorrelation* tool produces the output shown in Figure 4.8.

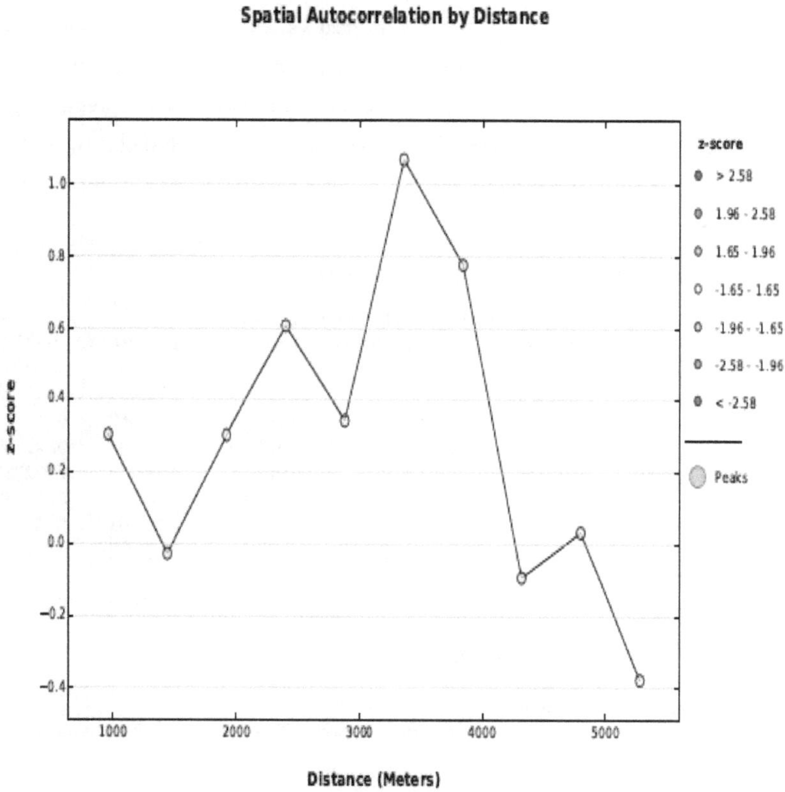

Figure 4.8: Spatial Autocorrelation by Distance

Results in Figure 4.8 shows that Spatial Autocorrelation calculated the number of neighbors per increment of 10 at a variety of distances while moving at 480 meters. It simply means that autocorrelation tool should run numerous times in order to find where the value is the highest. The starting point is 960 meters. The graph shows that the tool picks a point feature MBG then looks around the neighbor at 480 meters in order to find the distance at which clustering is intensified.

Figure 4.8 shows that the first and maximum peak values are non-existent. The z-score is at the level of deviation from the assumption of randomness. Comparing the level of statistical significance across various distances confirms that some z-scores are higher than others. Even though the peaks do not suggest natural that clustering of MBGs is maximized at any distance within the dataset. Findings are summarized in Table 4.1.

Table 4.1: Global Moran's I Summary by Distance

Global Moran's I Summary by Distance					
Distance	**Moran's Index**	**Expected Index**	**Variance**	**Z- Score**	**P-Value**
960.00*	0.02898	-0.029412	0.037212	0.032788	0.762052
1440.00*	-0.032608	-0.027778	0.029739	0.028011	0.977653
1920.00*	0.018409	-0.026316	0.022068	0.301069	0.763362
2400.00*	0.058857	-0.022727	0.017979	0.608449	0.542889
2880.00*	0.019769	-0.022222	0.015126	0.341429	0.732781
3360.00*	0.093832	-0.022222	0.011768	1.06983	0.284696
3840.00*	0.047007	-0.022222	0.007933	0.777063	0.437004
4320.00*	-0.02958	-0.022222	0.006048	-0.094608	0.924626
4800.00*	-0.019593	-0.021739	0.004638	0.031508	0.974865
5280.00*	-0.044666	-0.021739	0.00371	-0.376394	0.706624

First Peak (Distance, Value): None, None
Max Peak (Distance, Value): None, None
Distance measured in Meters
*At least one distance increment resulted in a feature with no neighbors which may invalidate the signficance of coreesponding results

Table 4.1 summarizes values of z-score from 10 peaks at an incremental distance of 480 meters. There is no maximum peak translating to non-existence of maximum clustering of MBGs in Thyolo district.

(c) Cluster and Outlier Analysis (Anselin Local Moran's I)

This tool creates a new feature class that analyses the clustering of MBGs based on number of farms while considering neighbors or otherwise. Figure 4.9 shows the map of MBGs in Thyolo district classified according to cluster.

Clustering and Outliers of MBGs in Thyolo District

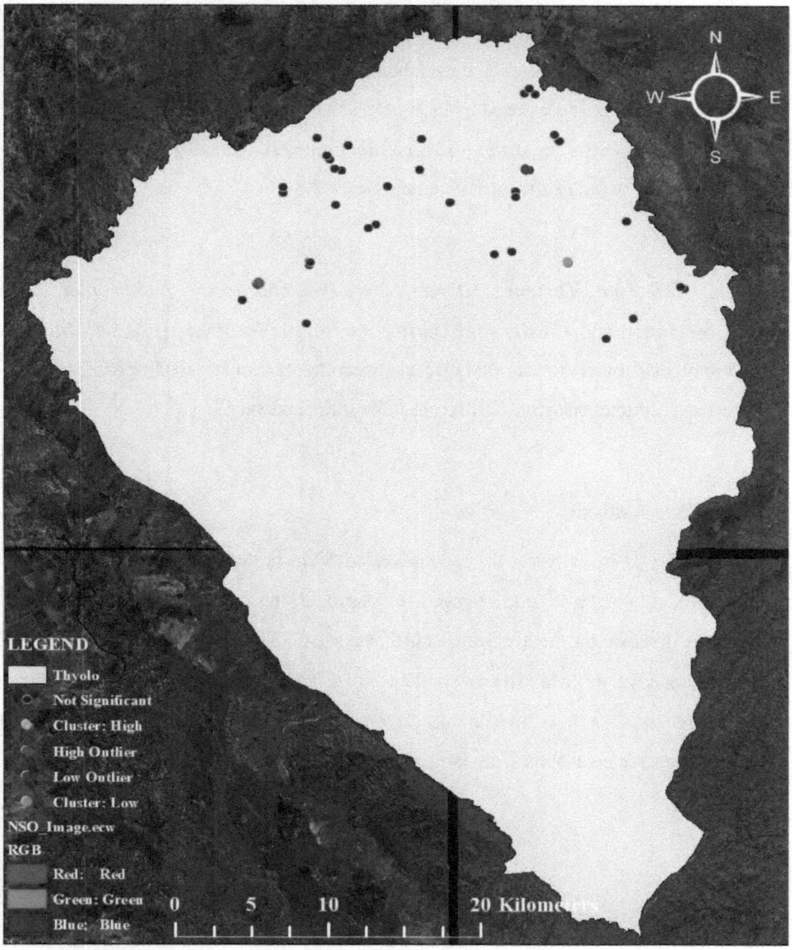

Figure 4.9: Map of MBGs Analyzed based on Clustering and Outliers

(C1) Cluster

The black points in Figure 4.9 indicate that there is no significant clustering, as z-scores are low while green points demonstrate features with similarly high values near each other. The distribution of green feature points means that MBGs have a high number of members close to each other. By contrast, the light blue points supposedly to have shown MBGs with low values/membership clustered near each other do not exist.

(C2) Outlier

The red and blue points on the map in Figure 4.9 are outliers. MBGs marked as red points have high memberships surrounded by MBGs with low memberships. Conversely, MBGs represented by blue points have low membership near high priority MBGs. Figure 4.13 demystifies the identification of statistically significant clustering and/or outliers in either low or high categories.

Tools *Calculate Distance Band from Neighborhood*, *Incremental Spatial Autocorrelation* and *Cluster and Outlier Analysis* reveal that farms and MBGs are randomly distributed in the study area. Meaning randomness of point features was achieved despite employing 3 different tools independently.

4.3.2 Buffer Analysis

Buffer Analysis investigates the recommended 8 km radius from the farm to the MBG. Therefore, it is imperative to engage the geoprocessing operator; buffer tool so that it measures distance outwardly from Namahoya MBG. The tool is based on input feature point Namahoya milk facility to create a buffer zone by specifying a linear unit of 8 km. Figure 4.10 depicts distribution pattern of farms that belong to Namahoya and buffer zone created around Namahoya MBG.

Distribution Pattern of Farms under Namahoya MBG

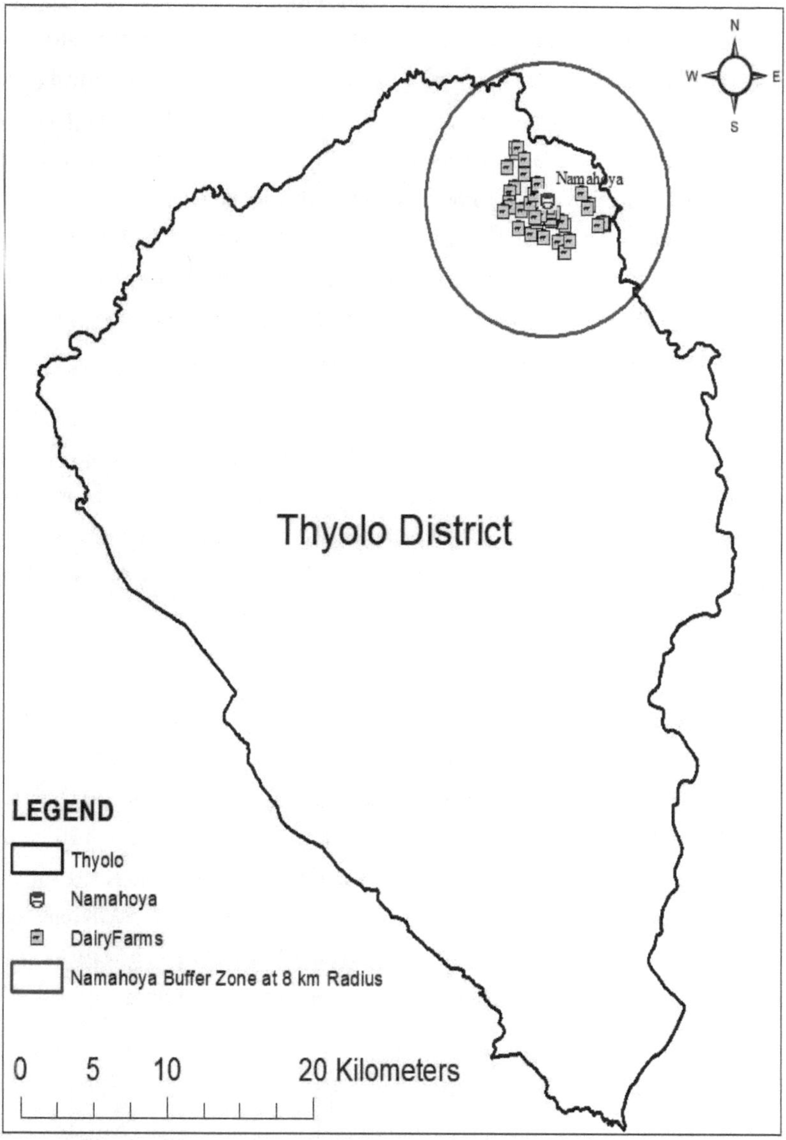

Figure 4.10: Distribution Pattern of Farms under Namahoya and Buffer Zone

A circular polygon is created with Namahoya highlighted blue in the middle. Findings indicate that 50 farmers are within the recommended 8 km radius from Namahoya MBG. However, Thyolo district has rivers, hills, meandering roads, private land among others as such using Euclidean distance would not reveal the actual traverse distances between farms and MBG. For example, to the east of Namahoya Figure 4.10, there are two large estates of Malawi University of Science and Technology and Ndata Farm. This means farmers who live further east of these estates go round to deliver the milk to Namahoya as trespassing is a crime in Malawi. Therefore, calculation of distances using Cartesian coordinates would not determine the recommended travel distance of 8 km radius. This necessitates engagement of road network using *route* analysis to determine travel distance and estimate travel time.

Furthermore, using buffer analysis, 50 sampled farms are investigated against all 48 MBGs to check nearness from each incident to milk facility. Buffer zones are created around 48 MBGs with input coverage feature specified distance at 8 km. This is to graphically assess positions of farms in a polygon. Depending on farm position in buffer zone, it becomes easier to conclude nearest MBG from the incident.

The process involves generation of buffer zones around each MBG. The buffer tool indicates that 50 farmers may supply milk to 8 different MBGs; namely Goliath, Goliati, Mwala Olemba, Nakhwakhwe, Ndata Amazing Grace, Namahoya, Okhalhavo and Super Dairy. Locations of farms (distances) from MBGs in Figure 4.16 indicate that 2% of farms are closest to Namahoya while 44 % are nearest to Ndata Amazing Grace. Nakhwakwe, Okhalhavo and Goliath has 3 farms in proximity each representing 18 % altogether. Supper Dairy and Golitai has 7 farms closest representing 14 % separately. The remaining 8 % of farms are nearest to Mwala Olemba.

4.3.3 Route Analysis

To find optimal routes, a network layer is employed. A network dataset layer consists of junctions showing total number of nodes and edges in a selected road network. Optimal route has varying meanings as it depends on impedance and one's intuition such as shortest distance, fastest route, number of highways, most scenic among myriad perceptions (*Route Analysis—ArcMap | Documentation*, 2021). The study has adopted time as impedance to solve route problem. Focus is on traversing shortest time possible to expedite milk transportation in order to minimize further milk deterioration.

Digitized road network (classified & unclassified roads) in Thyolo are 447.9 kilometers long in total with an estimated walking time of 89.57 hours at average speed 5 km/hour. Although the study involves other modes of transport such as bicycling and motorcycling, route analysis and closest analysis focus on walking which is commonest as revealed under *mode of transport* section by this study. In agreement to this revelation is the result by Palk et al. (2020) that assert that walking is the most (88%) used mode of transport in rural areas of Malawi. Therefore, the 5 km/hour was the adopted speed for farmers who walked to the MBG. The simulation is done in ArcMap representing the real world travel time and distance.

Running a new route in Network Analysis produces the quickest route between the source and destination. In this simulation, the route results between farm10 and Namahoya estimate that the farmer takes 0.86 hours to cover a distance of 4.35 km. Likewise; the model finds the shortest routes and calculates times taken against distances covered from all farms to Namahoya

Another notable finding worth mentioning is that farm14 is furthest from Namahoya having 14.8 km between two point features. This is the longest distance between the farm and the MBG from the set of farms. Farm14 is the only farm to be located beyond the threshold distance of 8 km. The remaining 49 farms are located not more than 8 kilometers from Namahoya.

Estimation of travel times and travel distances between two or more points is also possible using already existing technology such as google maps, google earth, mapline and others. For example, layers for farms and MBGs can be imported in google maps. Then transit time in relation to distances between farms and MBGs can be measured. Google maps finds shortest routes, approximates traverse times and distances using all modes of transport including trains and airplanes. This is an alternative as a farmer may just use a smart phone with an internet bundle from anywhere to query on the quickest route, travel time and distance. Ultimately, making the decision from the available information. However, one needs to capture coordinates for farms and MBGs (that are not readily available), create shape files and store them in a geodatabase for easy usage.

4.3.4 Closest Facility Analysis

In this context. the network layer selects the shortest route and determines nearest three MBGs from farm to MBG. The selection of routes and MBGs depends on least impedance. To use *Closest Facility* in transport model, incidents (farms) and facilities are loaded. Search tolerance of 8 km travel distance is used as impedance cutoff value.

The aim of loading farms and MBGs in ArcMap is to search for milk facilities that are located within the specified 8 km constraint. The 8 km is emanating from recommended radius of transporting unprocessed milk to avoid unacceptable levels of deterioration. In addition, among other parameters is target facility count that is set to three. Running *solve* function outputs shortest routes to three closest milk facilities.

Results display routes that each farmer can take to deliver milk to 3 nearest MBGs. For example, "FARM1" has Nansadi as nearest facility, then Mwala Olembe is nearer and Nakhwakhwe near. Closest Facility tool assigned Nansadi, Mwala Olemba and Nakhwakwe with digits 1,2 and 3 respectively to symbolize extent of proximity. Digit 1 being closest followed by 2 and finally 3. Furthermore, it was necessary to engage Query Builder.

(a) Query Builder

Query Builder improves visibility of shortest routes and nearest MBGs. It is used to filter incidents. Each farm is queried individually to find two quickest routes with corresponding MBGs. In this study, 2 was adopted but it can be any number. For example, by running a route tool in ArcMap, incident 10 determines two optimal routes with two MBG.

The data included geographical locations for farms and MBGs; land cover, land usage and road network. At this stage, identifying nearest facilities (MBGs) from incidents (farms) using the road network while considering land cover and land usage was tested using Closest Facility Analysis. FARM 10 had Goliath as its nearest MBG seconded by Goliati. There were no barriers in terms of point, line and polygons. As indicated earlier in this chapter, some farmers bypass their nearest MBGs to transport milk to Namahoya. Therefore, the Closest Facility tool provides capability of searching one or more nearest MBGs from every farm based on least travel distances. Relationship between farms to one nearest MBG is represented in Figure 4.11.

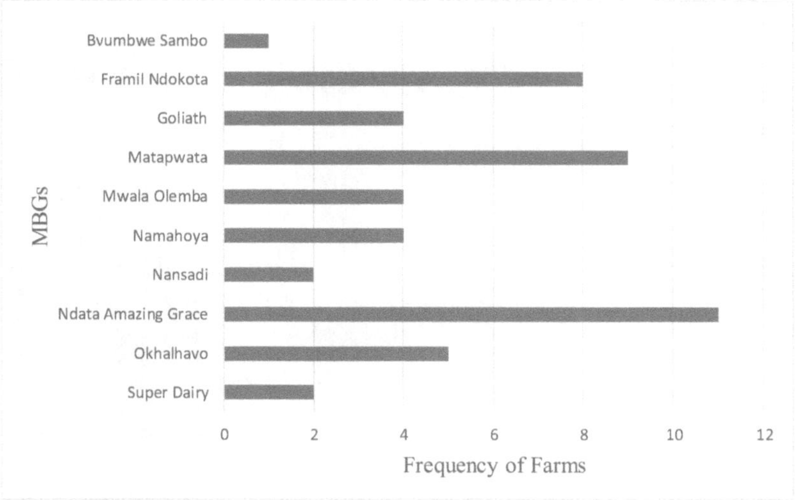

Figure 4.11: Frequency of Nearest Farm (s) to MBG

Taking into account dairy farms to their respective nearest facilities, results in Figure 4.20 indicate that 50 farms are nearest to 10 different MBGs and not only Namahoya as it suggests presently. Figure 4.20 shows that out of 50 farms that were sampled, only 8 % are located nearest to the facility and "eligible" to supply milk to Namahoya. The remaining, 92% of the farms are nearest to other nine different MBGs.

Closest facility confirms that 4% may be supply milk to Super Dairy whilst 4% to Nansadi MBGs. Bvumbwe Sambo MBG has 2% of farms nearest to it which is the lowest number while Ndata Amazing Grace has the highest number of nearest farms at 22 %. Those that bypass their nearest facility represent 92%. The remaining, 8% is in proximity with Namahoya. In the process, by-passer's time to deliver milk is elongated leading to further deterioration of milk.

(b) Total Time-Taken and Total Distance-Covered to Namahoya MBG

It is paramount to calculate total time taken and distance covered by all farmers from individual farms to Namahoya. Data from the attribute table is used to create a graph in Figure 4.12. The graph is created from an Excel worksheet.

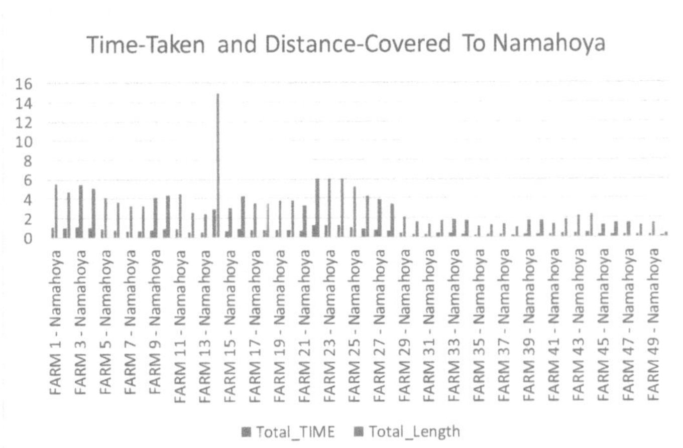

Figure 4.12: Time-Taken and Distance-Covered from 50 farms to Namahoya

The total estimated traverse time from all 50 incidents to Namahoya is 32.23 hours covering a total distance of 161.13 kilometers. The means for time and distance were 0.64 hours and 3.22 kilometers respectively. However, it is also necessary to estimate time taken to walk and distance covered to respective closest MBGs, and compare results.

(c) Total Time-Taken and Total Distance-Covered to Nearest MBG

Closest facility assessed time taken and distance covered by each farmer as shown in Figure 4.13.

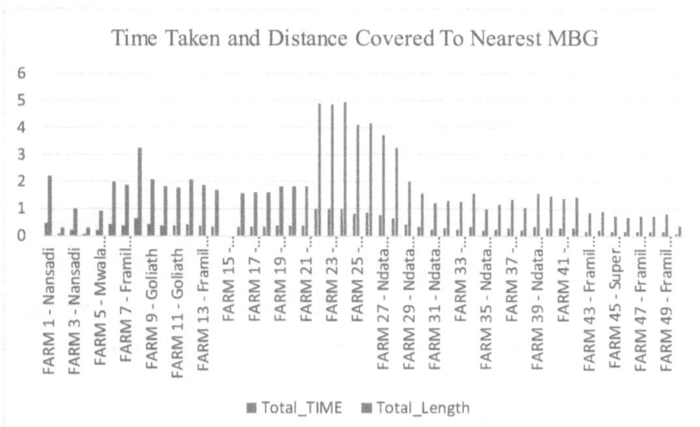

Figure 4.13: Time-Taken and Distance-Covered to Nearest MBG

When delivering milk to the nearest facility, findings estimate a sum of transit walking time to be 17.55 hours covering a total distance of 87.76 km. Averages for time taken and distance covered are 0.35 hours and 1.76 km for 50 smallholders. Therefore, transportation efficiency regarding total travel time and travel distances are compared between all 50 farmers when they deliver milk to Namahoya and when each farmer transports milk to their nearest facility.

By subtracting Total Travel Time Spent to Deliver Milk to Closest Facility (TTTSDMCF) from Total Travel Time Spent to Delivered Milk to Namahoya (TTTSDMN), using the formulae

$$\text{Time Difference} = \text{TTTSDMN} - \text{TTTSDMCF} \quad (4.1)$$

$$\text{So that} = 32.23 \text{ hours} - 17.56 \text{ hours} = 14.67 \text{ hours}$$

Since travel time varies directly with travel distance, it is necessary to examine differences in travel distances. This is when all farmers deliver milk to Namahoya (X) versus each farmer transporting milk to their respective nearest MBGs (Y).

$$\text{Distance Difference} = X - Y$$

$$= 161.13 \text{ km} - 87.76 \text{ km}$$

$$= 73.37 \text{ km}$$

Findings show that milk farmers took longer transit time and covered longer distances to get to Namahoya than to their closest MBGs. The difference in time and distance is a huge saving when milk is transported to the nearest MBG than when shipping it to Namahoya. The savings in terms of percentage were 45.52% and 45.53% for time and distance respectively. To improve transportation efficiencies, farmers with milk head loads can transport milk in lesser time and shorter distances to their nearest MBGs.

(d) Distances Covered to Namahoya by Each Farmer

The study compared farmers that operate within and outside 4 km travel distance taking into account milk volumes that are head-loaded and distance covered as variables. Time taken and distance covered is based on milk head loads that ranges between 7 liters and 10 liters for each farmer. Using the Closest Facility from all 50 facilities to Namahoya, the model calculated the distances and populated them in the attribute table of route layer. The partial snipped output is shown in Table 4.2.

Table 4.2: Distances between 50 incidents and Namahoya Considering Volume of Transported Milk

Table

Routes

ObjectID	Shape	FacilityID	FacilityRank	Name	IncidentCurbApproach	FacilityCurbApproach	IncidentID	Total_Length	Total_TIME
51	Polyline M	1	1	FARM 1 - Namahoya	Right side of vehicle	Left side of vehicle	1	5.499097	1.100107
52	Polyline M	1	1	FARM 2 - Namahoya	Right side of vehicle	Left side of vehicle	2	4.740509	0.94835
53	Polyline M	1	1	FARM 3 - Namahoya	Right side of vehicle	Left side of vehicle	3	5.488143	1.097916
54	Polyline M	1	1	FARM 4 - Namahoya	Right side of vehicle	Left side of vehicle	4	5.05154	1.010572
55	Polyline M	1	1	FARM 5 - Namahoya	Left side of vehicle	Left side of vehicle	5	4.131397	0.826495
56	Polyline M	1	1	FARM 6 - Namahoya	Right side of vehicle	Left side of vehicle	6	3.681145	0.736421
57	Polyline M	1	1	FARM 7 - Namahoya	Right side of vehicle	Left side of vehicle	7	3.26506	0.653183
58	Polyline M	1	1	FARM 8 - Namahoya	Right side of vehicle	Left side of vehicle	8	3.320267	0.664227
59	Polyline M	1	1	FARM 9 - Namahoya	Left side of vehicle	Left side of vehicle	9	4.071484	0.81451
60	Polyline M	1	1	FARM 10 - Namahoya	Right side of vehicle	Left side of vehicle	10	4.315882	0.863402
61	Polyline M	1	1	FARM 11 - Namahoya	Right side of vehicle	Left side of vehicle	11	4.458511	0.891935
62	Polyline M	1	1	FARM 12 - Namahoya	Right side of vehicle	Left side of vehicle	12	2.582297	0.516594
63	Polyline M	1	1	FARM 13 - Namahoya	Right side of vehicle	Left side of vehicle	13	2.380194	0.476163
64	Polyline M	1	1	FARM 14 - Namahoya	Left side of vehicle	Left side of vehicle	14	14.83689	2.968154
65	Polyline M	1	1	FARM 15 - Namahoya	Right side of vehicle	Left side of vehicle	15	3.068287	0.613818
66	Polyline M	1	1	FARM 16 - Namahoya	Right side of vehicle	Left side of vehicle	16	4.239966	0.848215
67	Polyline M	1	1	FARM 17 - Namahoya	Left side of vehicle	Left side of vehicle	17	3.567192	0.713625
68	Polyline M	1	1	FARM 18 - Namahoya	Right side of vehicle	Left side of vehicle	18	3.554604	0.711107
69	Polyline M	1	1	FARM 19 - Namahoya	Right side of vehicle	Left side of vehicle	19	3.707891	0.741772
70	Polyline M	1	1	FARM 20 - Namahoya	Left side of vehicle	Left side of vehicle	20	3.707891	0.741772
71	Polyline M	1	1	FARM 21 - Namahoya	Right side of vehicle	Left side of vehicle	21	3.285643	0.6573
72	Polyline M	1	1	FARM 22 - Namahoya	Right side of vehicle	Left side of vehicle	22	6.051312	1.210579
73	Polyline M	1	1	FARM 23 - Namahoya	Left side of vehicle	Left side of vehicle	23	5.995701	1.199454
74	Polyline M	1	1	FARM 24 - Namahoya	Right side of vehicle	Left side of vehicle	24	6.070823	1.214482
75	Polyline M	1	1	FARM 25 - Namahoya	Right side of vehicle	Left side of vehicle	25	5.239709	1.048216
76	Polyline M	1	1	FARM 26 - Namahoya	Right side of vehicle	Left side of vehicle	26	4.272596	0.854743
77	Polyline M	1	1	FARM 27 - Namahoya	Left side of vehicle	Left side of vehicle	27	3.840074	0.768216
78	Polyline M	1	1	FARM 28 - Namahoya	Right side of vehicle	Left side of vehicle	28	3.341918	0.668558
79	Polyline M	1	1	FARM 29 - Namahoya	Right side of vehicle	Left side of vehicle	29	2.084363	0.416982
80	Polyline M	1	1	FARM 30 - Namahoya	Left side of vehicle	Left side of vehicle	30	1.648214	0.329729
81	Polyline M	1	1	FARM 31 - Namahoya	Left side of vehicle	Left side of vehicle	31	1.323281	0.264725
82	Polyline M	1	1	FARM 32 - Namahoya	Left side of vehicle	Left side of vehicle	32	1.766088	0.35331
83	Polyline M	1	1	FARM 33 - Namahoya	Left side of vehicle	Left side of vehicle	33	1.812649	0.362625
84	Polyline M	1	1	FARM 34 - Namahoya	Right side of vehicle	Left side of vehicle	34	1.668585	0.333804
85	Polyline M	1	1	FARM 35 - Namahoya	Left side of vehicle	Left side of vehicle	35	1.075125	0.215081
86	Polyline M	1	1	FARM 36 - Namahoya	Right side of vehicle	Left side of vehicle	36	1.27528	0.255123
87	Polyline M	1	1	FARM 37 - Namahoya	Right side of vehicle	Left side of vehicle	37	1.343209	0.268712
88	Polyline M	1	1	FARM 38 - Namahoya	Right side of vehicle	Left side of vehicle	38	1.031847	0.206423
89	Polyline M	1	1	FARM 39 - Namahoya	Left side of vehicle	Left side of vehicle	39	1.668585	0.333804

Some of the results in Table 4.2 are distance covered and time taken to deliver milk to Namahoya by individual dairy farmers. Relating distances to milk volumes that are head-loaded indicates that those that operate from >= 4 km distance ferry less milk quantities compared to those that cover a distance of <4. The reason is that walking with heavier load on the head (larger milk volumes) causes delay in transporting milk to the MBG. The discovery concurs with a study by Lucas-Cuevas et al. (2013) that walking with load carriage reduces speed. Subsequently, the milk deteriorates leading to rejection often times.

Furthermore, using regression analysis, results from face-to-face interviews indicate that those that bicycled to Namahoya transport relatively more milk quantities than those that walk despite milking equal quantities at times. For example, farmers that operate from FARM23 (bicycled) and FARM24 (walked) and are situated adjacent to each other. The former produces 12 liters while the later produces 13 liters. A farmer from FARM23 transports a minimum of 10 liters daily while the one from FARM24 carries a maximum of 7 liters. This significant difference is influenced by mode of transport.

So far, the analysis is based on one incident to one facility relationship. In reality, one incident to many facilities is also feasible. It is a function of indicating a desired number of facilities to find under *Analysis Settings* tab in ArcMap. In this example, 3 is used to search for 3 nearest MBGs that are ranked 1, 2 and 3. However, it can be any number. The snipped Table 4.3 shows the resultant output in the attribute table.

Table 4.3: Three Closest MBGs from Every Farm

Table

Routes

ObjectID	Shape	FacilityID	FacilityRank	Name	IncidentCurbApproach	FacilityCurbApproach	IncidentID	Total_Length
1	Polyline M	5	1	FARM 1 - Nansadi	Right side of vehicle	Right side of vehicle	1	2.210514
2	Polyline M	4	2	FARM 1 - Mwala Olemba	Right side of vehicle	Left side of vehicle	1	2.249616
3	Polyline M	6	3	FARM 1 - Nakhwakhwe	Right side of vehicle	Right side of vehicle	1	3.030373
4	Polyline M	4	1	FARM 2 - Mwala Olemba	Left side of vehicle	Left side of vehicle	2	0.272804
5	Polyline M	5	2	FARM 2 - Nansadi	Left side of vehicle	Right side of vehicle	2	0.549212
6	Polyline M	6	3	FARM 2 - Nakhwakhwe	Left side of vehicle	Right side of vehicle	2	1.738763
7	Polyline M	5	1	FARM 3 - Nansadi	Right side of vehicle	Right side of vehicle	3	0.95813
8	Polyline M	4	2	FARM 3 - Mwala Olemba	Right side of vehicle	Left side of vehicle	3	1.234538
9	Polyline M	6	3	FARM 3 - Nakhwakhwe	Right side of vehicle	Right side of vehicle	3	1.77799
10	Polyline M	4	1	FARM 4 - Mwala Olemba	Right side of vehicle	Right side of vehicle	4	0.261579
11	Polyline M	5	2	FARM 4 - Nansadi	Right side of vehicle	Right side of vehicle	4	0.537987
12	Polyline M	6	3	FARM 4 - Nakhwakhwe	Right side of vehicle	Right side of vehicle	4	1.727538
13	Polyline M	4	1	FARM 5 - Mwala Olemba	Right side of vehicle	Left side of vehicle	5	0.881916
14	Polyline M	5	2	FARM 5 - Nansadi	Right side of vehicle	Right side of vehicle	5	1.158324
15	Polyline M	6	3	FARM 5 - Nakhwakhwe	Right side of vehicle	Right side of vehicle	5	2.347876
16	Polyline M	4	1	FARM 6 - Mwala Olemba	Right side of vehicle	Left side of vehicle	6	1.962337
17	Polyline M	5	2	FARM 6 - Nansadi	Right side of vehicle	Right side of vehicle	6	2.238745
18	Polyline M	30	3	FARM 6 - Framil Ndokota	Left side of vehicle	Right side of vehicle	6	2.998177
19	Polyline M	30	1	FARM 7 - Framil Ndokota	Right side of vehicle	Right side of vehicle	7	1.865858
20	Polyline M	4	2	FARM 7 - Mwala Olemba	Left side of vehicle	Left side of vehicle	7	2.848348
21	Polyline M	7	3	FARM 7 - Goliath	Right side of vehicle	Left side of vehicle	7	3.025905
22	Polyline M	10	1	FARM 8 - Ndata Amazing Grace	Right side of vehicle	Right side of vehicle	8	3.239527
23	Polyline M	1	2	FARM 8 - Namahoya	Right side of vehicle	Left side of vehicle	8	3.320267
24	Polyline M	9	3	FARM 8 - Super Dairy	Right side of vehicle	Right side of vehicle	8	3.326635
25	Polyline M	7	1	FARM 9 - Goliath	Left side of vehicle	Left side of vehicle	9	2.067488
26	Polyline M	2	2	FARM 9 - Goliati	Left side of vehicle	Left side of vehicle	9	2.102315
27	Polyline M	30	3	FARM 9 - Framil Ndokota	Left side of vehicle	Right side of vehicle	9	2.672282
28	Polyline M	7	1	FARM 10 - Goliath	Right side of vehicle	Left side of vehicle	10	1.814067
29	Polyline M	2	2	FARM 10 - Goliati	Right side of vehicle	Left side of vehicle	10	1.848894
30	Polyline M	8	3	FARM 10 - Okhalhavo	Right side of vehicle	Right side of vehicle	10	2.655133
31	Polyline M	7	1	FARM 11 - Goliath	Right side of vehicle	Left side of vehicle	11	1.750824
32	Polyline M	2	2	FARM 11 - Goliati	Right side of vehicle	Left side of vehicle	11	1.78565
33	Polyline M	8	3	FARM 11 - Okhalhavo	Right side of vehicle	Right side of vehicle	11	2.591889
34	Polyline M	30	1	FARM 12 - Framil Ndokota	Right side of vehicle	Right side of vehicle	12	2.052239
35	Polyline M	7	2	FARM 12 - Goliath	Right side of vehicle	Left side of vehicle	12	2.1008
36	Polyline M	2	3	FARM 12 - Goliati	Right side of vehicle	Left side of vehicle	12	2.135627
37	Polyline M	30	1	FARM 13 - Framil Ndokota	Right side of vehicle	Right side of vehicle	13	1.850137
38	Polyline M	7	2	FARM 13 - Goliath	Right side of vehicle	Left side of vehicle	13	1.898697
39	Polyline M	2	3	FARM 13 - Goliati	Right side of vehicle	Left side of vehicle	13	1.933524

This means that the model manages to find 3 nearest MBGs from each farm. For example, drawing from the results in the attribute Table 4.3, farml has Nansadi as its closest MBG, then Mwala Olembe and finally Nakhwakwe. The digits 1, 2 and 3 in variable *FacilityRank* implies that the first choice (nearest) facility is Nansadi. If the nearest facility is not buying milk due to any reason, then the second nearest facility is Mwala Olemba. If the second MBG is not buying milk, then the third option for farml is Nakhwakwe. Priority is determined by time-based cost attribute as impedance in relation to distance.

IncidentCurbApproach modelled a route for approaching a stop at MBG from a particular side based on edge direction of the farm. Farmers approached the MBG on the door side where milk is received for testing. On the other hand, FacilityCurbApproach indicated side of the MBG to a farmer when arriving or departing the milk facility.

(e) Frequency Distribution of Time and Distance

Using ArcMap statistical function to examine routes, the function produces statistical results shown in Figures 4.14 and 4.15. The examination is based on both time and distance as variables.

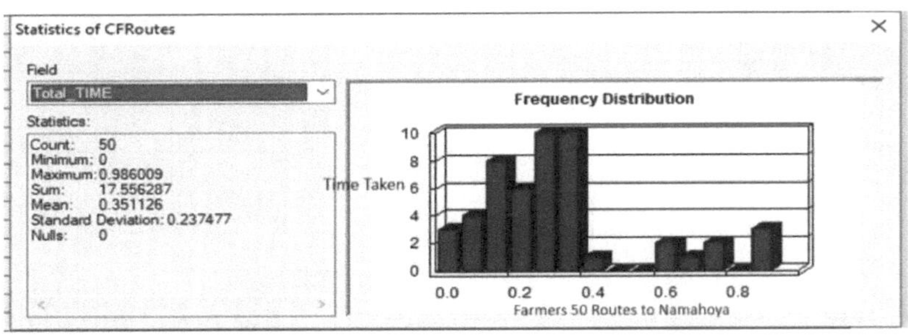

Figure 4.14: Statistics on Routes Based on Time

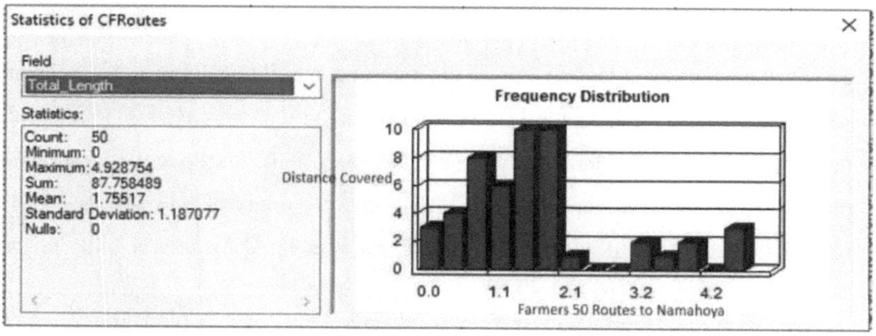

Figure 4.15: Statistics on Routes Based on Distance

Closest Facility examines the extent to which findings by Route Analysis are similar or different to each other. Figures 4.14 and 4.15 show that frequency distribution is the same. Meaning that there is a direct proportion between time taken and distance covered.

Time is a dependent variable recorded as traverse time on each of the 50 routes between 50 different farms and Namahoya. The estimated hours that 50 farmers would take to cover the routes are 17.56 with a mean of 0.35 hours and a standard deviation of 0.24 hours. Translation of 0.24 hours as standard deviation is that the values are clustered towards the mean. The statistics on time varies directly to distance as a variable. The total sum of distance for 50 routes is 87.76 km averaging 1.76 km with a standard deviation of 1.19 km. The value of standard deviation which is 1.19 is an indication that the set of values on distance are dispersed.

In this study, both Closest Facility analysis and Route Analysis calculated and provided exact results in terms of finding quickest route, time taken and distance covered. Using the two Network Analyst tools, the model provides empirical findings than one can rely on. Related work by Kharel and Shivananda, (2018) from Bangalore in India reports that the same tools were utilized to model routes, find optimal routes and find nearest gas stations. Meaning that employing the two tools, one can find any kind of facility from the incident be it a hospital, school and others.

4.3.5 Transport Model

The third objective was to develop a spatial transport model to determine optimal routes when delivering unprocessed milk. Route is concerned with a polyline(s) joining more than one location. In this study, route involves milk transportation through a polyline/road that connects farms and MBGs. It was paramount to interview farmers first if they understood time taken and distance covered to deliver milk to their respective MBGs. Results are tabulated in Figure 4.16.

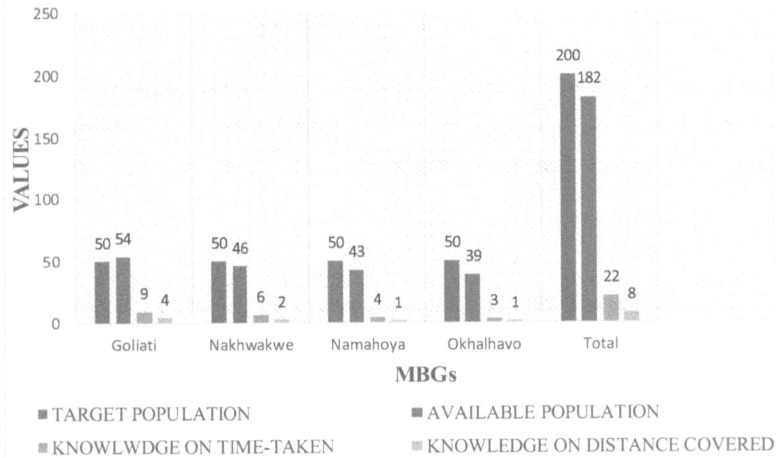

Figure 4.16: Statistics on Questionnaire

The questionnaire was administered with farmers from Goliati, Nakhwakwe and Namahoya. The study targeted 50 farmers from each of the 4 MBGs. The available population for Goliati exceeded by 4 participants while Nakhwakwe was less by the same margin. Namahoya had 43 participants and Okhalhavo registered 39 participants. Out of the 200 targeted respondents, 92 % were available. Only 12 % and 4.1 % were able to estimate time taken and distance travelled respectively from farms to their particular MBGs. Generally, this showed little knowledge on metrics involved between farms and MBGs.

This necessitated calculation of time-taken with corresponding distance covered between the farm and MBG in relation to their mode of transport on the road network. The transport model was designed and represented in a flow chart Figure 3.6 (Methodology section). Sequence of processes were connected to show workflows in the transport model. Road network and Land Cover were converted to raster format. The reason is that calculation of time and distance works in this format. There was little known information on average speeds when one is walking, bicycling or motorcycling with load. In this study, the load is the volume of milk that is delivered from farm to MBG. Therefore, the model adopted conventional average speeds for walking, bicycling and motorcycling as 5 km/hour, 20 km/hour and 30 km/hour respectively (Atkins, 2017).

How to optimize routes when transporting milk from a farm to a MBG through spatial analysis approach was the research question of this study. Therefore, it was necessary to calculate travel time and travel distance so that farmers should make informed decisions before setting out to deliver milk. The transport model used time as cost in order to find the shortest route and corresponding distance of a trip in a road network. In order to analyze the selected points (farm and MBG), *a solve* function was executed where the output displayed distance covered between points and estimated travel time based on mode of transport (foot, bicycle, motorcycle).

4.4 Chapter Summary

The chapter discussed results when transporting unprocessed milk from farm to MBG by employing spatial analysis approach. It presented findings on distribution pattern incidents and facilities by using spatial autocorrelation. More so, it assessed if the farms are located within the recommended 8 km radius or outside from the MBG by engaging proximity tool; buffer analysis. Road network connected farms and MBGs. It was used to estimate travel time and determine travel distance. Closest facility provided least distance from farm to two MBGs. Finally, the transport model showed the workflows in a flow chart for easy understanding using one output process as input of another.

CHAPTER 5: CONCLUSION AND RECOMMENDATION

The study optimized routes when transporting unprocessed milk from farm to MBG through spatial analysis approach in Thyolo district, Malawi. The study mapped geographical locations of farms and MBGs on earth's surface. It also revealed that the point features are randomly distributed. Based on Euclidean distance, the study uncovered that 50 sampled farms were located within the recommended radius of 8 km despite having no farmer traversing in a straight line to MBG. Information such as travel time, travel distance, shortest route and closest facility was made available to farmers in form of printouts for informed decision-making. Time as impedance was adopted to find shortest routes with a motive of minimizing milk deterioration.

Overall, this study is different to earlier similar studies that solved transportation problems in terms of point features and road networks. Previous studies considered milk transportation from MBG to the milk processing plant where roads connecting them are mostly tarmacked. Also, tankers/vehicles that ferry unprocessed milk in bulk using well established roads were taken into consideration. To the contrary, in this study, the transport problem started from the farm and ended at the milk collection center. Additionally, edges that connect farms and MBGs are paths that are narrow. These paths are only used for footing, bicycling and motorcycling as tankers or any other vehicles cannot fit in due to the nature of the terrain.

5.1 Conclusion

The assessment and optimization of transportation of unprocessed milk from the farm to the MBG was probably the first in Malawi. The investigation included farms that are located away from classified roads. Farmers use feeder paths to get to classified roads that are used when solving the most researched VRP. These feeder paths are narrower in width that are only used by pedestrians, bicyclists and motorcyclists. Furthermore, the study considered the milk farmer who is the source in the dairy industry value chain. Thereafter, GIS technology was employed particularly Spatial Autocorrelation, Buffer Analysis, Route Analysis and Closest Facility Analysis to assess and optimize transportation problem spatially.

5.1.1 Spatial Autocorrelation

Spatial Autocorrelation helped to understand the distribution pattern of MBGs as point features and their relationships with allied nearby features. The function showed that MBGs were dispersed and the number of farmers from each milk collection point varied. For example, Namahoya had 353 members while Nakhwakwe, a nearby feature, had 150 members thus a huge gap. To the contrary, Namahoya had 353 farmers and Goliati, the adjacent MBG had 385 members. The difference in membership for these two nearby objects was not huge as compared to Namahoya-Nakhwakhwe membership relationship. This proved inequality of membership base despite being in proximity.

5.1.2 Buffer Analysis

Buffer geoprocessing tool analyzed the recommended 8 km radius between 50 farms and Namahoya milk collection center. All the 50 farms were located within a distance of 8 km. One would assume that there are straight roads or paths from the 50 farms to Namahoya which is an unrealistic representation. For example, to the east of Namahoya, there are private estates such as Ndata farm and Malawi University of Science and Technology (MUST) covering huge areas. So, to avoid trespassing, farmers who operate further east of these 2 estates have to go round them in order to deliver milk to Namahoya. Therefore, it is this land cover and land usage that makes the statement of *recommended radius of 8 km* to be inappropriate.

Therefore, this study proposes that "*recommended 8 km radius*" that most previous studies quoted be replaced with "*recommended traverse distance of 8 km*". Distance travelled by farmers from the farm to the MBG is more meaningful than the radius between the farm and the MBG. This problem was solved using either *route tool* or *Closest Facility Analysis* in ArcGIS that calculated actual traverse distance.

5.1.3 Route Analysis

Route in ArcMap allowed performing spatial analysis on Thyolo road network. Particularly finding shortest routes, estimation of transit times and calculations of distances between farms and MBGs. This helped farmers to make informed decisions by deciding what time to depart the farm for MBG since they would estimate traverse time based on shortest distance.

Prior to this study, information on distances travelled and time taken was sketchy, thus making it difficult for farmers to plan transportation of their unprocessed milk. Using observation as a data collection tool, it was discerned that most neither owned computers nor smartphones where they could query the system on shortest distance, estimation of transit time, locate nearest MBG and find shortest route. This prompted printing of thematic maps and giving every farmer. The maps graphically showed shortest route, estimated transit time, traverse distance and showed nearest MBG from the farm. This was to empower farmers with information so that informed decisions are made in relation to milk delivery.

5.1.4 Closest Facility Analysis

Modelling the transport system to find the nearest facility from any incident was possible with the use of Closest Facility Analysis. The tool identified the nearest facility based on the least time and distance. The tool showed that travel times and travel distances were significantly reduced as it revealed that 50 farms were nearest to 10 different MBGs and not to Namahoya MBG. This would support delivery of less-deteriorated milk and likely to be accepted at MBGs. Eventually, there would positive outcome in the form of revenue to smallholder dairy farmers.

5.1.5 Transport Model

Transport modelling constituted connecting farms with MBGs through a road network to solve a real transport problem in milk supply chain. The model estimated travel time based on mode of transport and calculated distances between farms and MBGs. Furthermore, it managed to find quickest route and closest milk facility for each of the 50 farms. Therefore, the model addressed the real problems for dairy farmers.

5.2 Recommendations

The study makes recommendations to smallholder dairy farmers, MBGs, Government of Malawi and academic institutions.

5.2.1 Smallholder Dairy Farmer

Since the majority of farmers transport milk on foot to the MBG, the study recommends that farmers should mobilize themselves and benefit from free buffalo bicycles offered by World Bicycle Relief. In Malawi, the world Organization is already supporting some dairy farmers so that they switch from walking to bicycling. Meaning that farmers should upgrade from milk head-loading to carrying milk on bicycles. For example, one farmer switched from walking to bicycling when delivering milk to the MBG, his daily milk load capacity doubled and subsequently the monthly income improved (*Dairy Farmer Goes Stronger With His Buffalo Bicycle – World Bicycle Relief*, 2021)

In addition, farmers need to be trained on how to make queries in GIS platform so that they can select shortest paths and identify closest MBGs. Therefore, farmers should own a smartphone/computer in order to use the spatial transport model so that they approximate time and distance involved to a specific MBG. This would help them to make instant decisions regarding delivery of milk.

5.2.2 MBG

Milk buyers actively run day-to-day operations of this entity. This study, therefore, recommends to the committee that milk buyers should be trained in basic GIS operations so that they should be able to query ArcMap of quickest route, least traverse time, calculations of distance, query on nearest facility and printing/reprinting of related maps. When executive committee is employing new *milk buyers*, the researcher recommends recruiting candidates with basic computer knowledge as it would be less expensive to train them on GIS. Furthermore, efficient communication would be made easy between the GIS transport model designer and end-users in an event that remote support is required.

5.2.3 Government of Malawi

A more affordable and efficient way to transport milk is by bicycling rather than walking. Delivery of milk as head-load by farmer on foot enables spending more time on the road and wasting more energy. Therefore, this study recommends that the Government of Malawi provide loans in form of bicycles so that there is improvement in milk volumes delivery. Increased quantities of milk transported translates to improved payoffs to smallholder farmers.

5.2.4 Academic Institutions

It was difficult to consult other people conversant with GIS for third opinion besides the academic supervisor. The researcher discovered that people with GIS specialization are rare in Malawi. Therefore, this study proposes that educational institutions in collaboration with the Government of Malawi should strategize on developing adequate GIS human resource.

5.3 Study Contributions

This section outlines study contributions, sub-categorized into theoretical and practical ones.

5.3.1 Theoretical Contributions

The study employed Decision Theory in order to assess transportation of unprocessed milk from the farm to the MBG using spatial analysis approach. Decision Theory in collaboration with GIS helped to understand the intricacies encompassed in the milk transportation system and making of informed logistical decisions by the smallholder dairy farmer.

Drawing from the theory, construct *Acts* were farmers who decided departure time from the farm considering the mode of transport to get to the milk collection center. ArcMap revealed the distances from every farm to MBG and estimated transit times per individual farmer. In the event that a farmer faced an eventuality like un-purchasing of milk by the MBG due to some reason, the model provided a second and third option. The uncertainty resulted in delivering milk to the next MBG if the first choice was not servicing. Otherwise, the farmer would get the milk back home for consumption, hence the negative *outcome*.

Buffer Analysis tool indicated that farms were located within the recommended 8 km radius. However, no single farmer used the radius to deliver the unprocessed milk due to non –existence of straight-line roads/paths between the farm and MBG. Land usage showed that there are houses, gardens, private land among others. Hence, the proposal to replace the phrase *recommended 8 km radius* with *recommended travel distance of 8 km*. This contribution is an addition to the body of research.

5.3.2 Practical Contribution

The study mapped 48 MBGs in Thyolo district and 50 farms from Namahoya that have since been uploaded on google maps platform (See Appendix J) with the intention of making features public and usable by anyone from any location on earth. The same mapping can also be viewed on Google Earth. Farmers and everyone can locate geographical locations and distribution patterns of features. Subsequently, farmers can find the quickest route to MBG, calculate travel time and travel distance between point locations. More so, a milk spatial transport that was modelled, selected optimal routes based on least travel time in relation to least travel distances between the farm and the MBG.

The transport model that constituted was designed using an evolutionary approach so that future researchers can use it beyond the scope of this study. It included use of Buffer Analysis, Spatial Autocorrelation, Route Analysis and Closest Facility Analysis. This study informs subsequent GIS projects on how to map any point feature classes, incorporate them in google maps so that they are accessed worldwide and solve any transportation problem using spatial analysis approach beyond the milk industry. This entails that not only can this approach be used in this or similar scope but also in other areas of application.

5.4 Study Limitations

There were several restrictions along the way but the major ones were -

5.4.1 Extra Costs on Operations

The researcher physically visited MBGs in order to capture coordinates and conduct face to face interviews with some dairy farmers. In some cases, travelling from one MBG to the next resulted in finding them closed for business as they are sparsely distributed. The researcher had to rely on neighboring homes to ask for contacts for MBGs leaders. MBGs operate from 5 hours to unscheduled varying closing time. As earlier mentioned under methodology chapter, SHMPA gave out an outdated "phonebook". During field visits, the researcher discovered that other MBGs existed in Thyolo under a grouping called FAMPA.

More so, getting directions and locations of the next MBG from smallholder dairy farmers or people the researcher met along the way was also a challenge. In the process, the researcher skipped some MBGs unknowingly. This was rectified by visiting the District Animal Health and Livestock Development Officer who provided a full list of MBGs in Thyolo. The list included MBGs from both SHMPA and FAMPA. The officer provided directions that led to locations of "missed" MBGs. Consequently, this led to unbudgeted transport expenditure.

5.4.2 Coronavirus Disease 2019

The other limitation was Corona Virus Disease 2019 that wreaked havoc around the globe. The pandemic contributed to delay in data collection since Government agencies, private institutions were operating in shifts, and others were closed completely. To reduce further delay in engaging respondents, the researcher resorted to making voice/WhatsApp video calls to introduce the topic and convince them so that they share data electronically or allow the visit physically while adhering to preventive measures. Consequently, thesis completion took longer than the scheduled 12 months, as it was a challenge to maneuver and collect data from the targeted population and institutions.

5.5 Further Research

This study dwelt on optimizing routes when transporting unprocessed milk through spatial analysis approach. The focus was on spatial distribution patterns of farms and MBGs; finding shortest routes between incidents and facilities; and finding nearest facility for dairy farmers. Therefore, future scholars may attempt to investigate transportation of unprocessed milk by considering impediments such as road turns, time windows, restrictions, historical traffic data and land elevation. This would give a more detailed result.

Additionally, dairy industry has numerous un-researched areas that future researchers may consider when solving transport problems using GIS. For example, at the time of field visits, the researcher observed how records were stored as shown in Figure 5.1. This type of record keeping may result in losing important information. GIS supports Database Management Systems (DBMS) such as PostgreSQL, MySQL, Oracle and others. Therefore, farmers' records may be stored and retrieved in DBMS using GIS. Secondly, when the secretariat (MBG) wanted to give an update on any item to farmers, the communication was through the notice board as shown in Figure 5.2. This means that the farmer has to travel physically to the MBG to access any update when we are in a digital world. Therefore, future researchers may attempt to use GIS in solving such problems.

5.5.1 Record Keeping

Figure 5.1 Diaries kept at Goliati MBG

At Goliati MBG, 5 farmers' dairies were kept unattended on the open table while 2 dairies were hidden in the coverless electricity main switch box. These milk dairies are supposed to be in custody of farmers by carrying them to their homes and bringing them with them when delivering the milk so that quantities received are recorded. On the contrary, they are kept at the MBG.

5.5.2 Communication

Figure 5.2: Notice at Dwale MBG on notice board

The notice is inscribed in Chichewa language, Malawi's national language, it reads "*Notice, buy solar lamps and wireless radios on credit at affordable prices on 3 monthly installments, thank you, management*". This implies that the smallholder farmer had to physically visit Dwale MBG to know of the credit facility or hear it from the MBG-mate when in contact.

5.6 Chapter Summary

The chapter concluded by recapping the roles that spatial autocorrelation, buffer analysis, route analysis and closest facility played in this study. Thereafter recommendations were made to smallholder dairy farmers, MBGs, government of Malawi and academic institutions. Contributions were highlighted and future scholars were tipped on areas of further research.

REFERENCES

Abousaeidi, M., Fauzi, R., & Muhamad, R. (2016). Determining efficient delivery routes in specific time-frames using Geographic Information System. *Journal of Environmental Biology*, *37*(5), 1167.

Ahmed, Z. U., Krupnik, T. J., & Kamal, M. (2018). *Introduction to basic GIS and spatial analysis using QGIS: Applications in Bangladesh*. Cereal Systems Initiative for South Asia (CSISA) and the International Maize and Wheat Improvement Center, CIMMYT.

Alam, B. M. (2012). *Application of Geographic Information Systems*. InTech. www.intechopen.com////http://dx.doi.org/10.5772/1944

Ali, J. (2012). Factors Affecting the Adoption of Information and Communication Technologies (ICTs) for Farming Decisions. *Journal of Agricultural & Food Information*, 78–96. https://doi.org/10.1080/10496505.2012.636980

Allen, D. W., & Coffey, J. M. (2019). *Focus on Geodatabases in ArcGIS Pro*. Esri Press.

Atkins, W. (2017). *Malawi National Transport Master Plan*. Ministry of Transport and Public Works of Malawi.

Babbie, E. (2013). *The Practice of Social Research* (13th Edition).

Bajjali, W. (2018). *Geodatabase. In: ArcGIS for Environmental and Water Issues*. Springer, Cham. ttps://doi.org/10.1007/978-3-319-61158-7_7

Banda, L. J., Gondwe, T. N., Gausi, W., Masangano, C., Fatch, P., Wellard, K., Banda, J. W., & Kaunda, E. W. (2011). *Challenges and Opportunities of Smallholder*

Dairy Production Systems: A Case Study of Selected Districts in Malawi. University of Malawi: Bunda College of Agriculture.

Barnard, J. (2006). *Milk enterprise development in Malawi*.

Bolstad, P. (2016). *GIS Fundamentals: A First Text on Geographic Information Systems* (5th ed.). Eider Press.

Bosona, T., Nordmark, I., Gebresenbet, G., & Ljungberg, D. (2013). *GIS-Based Analysis of Integrated Food Distribution Network in Local Food Supply Chain. Vol. 8*. https://doi.org/doi:10.5539/ijbm.v8n17p13

Bowen, G. (2009). Document Analysis as a Qualitative Research Method. *Qualitative Research Journal*, *9*, 27–40. https://doi.org/10.3316/QRJ0902027

Braekers, K., Ramaekers, K., & Van Nieuwenhuyse, I. (2016). The vehicle routing problem: State of the art classification and review. *Computers & Industrial Engineering*, *99*, 300–313. https://doi.org/10.1016/j.cie.2015.12.007

Brunsdon, C., & Comber, L. (2015). *An Introduction to R for Spatial Analysis and Mapping*. SAGE Publications Ltd.

Budai, B. (2020). *Exploring the Ways of Providing High Service Quality at Low Cost in the Economy Hotel Sector* [University of East London Royal Docks School of Business and Law]. https://repository.uel.ac.uk/item/889wy

Charikar, M., Khuller, S., Mount, D. M., & Narasimhan, G. (2001). Algorithms for Facility Location Problems with Outliers. *ACM-SIAM Symposium on Discrete Algorithms*, 642–651. https://www.cs.umd.edu/~mount/Papers/soda01-outlier.pdf

Chaudhary, V., Kulshrestha, R., & Routroy, S. (2018). State-of-the-art literature review on inventory models for perishable products. *Journal of Advances in Management Research*, *15*(3), 306–346. https://doi.org/10.1108/JAMR-09-2017-0091

Chitika, R. (2008). *Marketing Channel Choice: Its Determinants and Evaluation of Transaction Costs in Smallholder Dairy Farming in Lilongwe Milkshed Area Malawi*. University of Malawi.

Creswell, J. W. (2014). *Research design: Qualitative, quantitative, and mixed methods approaches* (4th Edition). SAGE Publications, Inc.

Creswell, J. W., & Clark, V. L. P. (2018). *Designing and Conducting Mixed Methods Research* (3rd Edition). SAGE Publications, Inc.

Da-bing, H., & Jian-chuan, L. (2010). *Study on the Optional Route Algorithm of the ArcGIS Network-Based Improved Road Traffic*. Second International Conference on Networks Security, Wireless Communications and Trusted Computing.

Dairy Farmer Goes Stronger With His Buffalo Bicycle – World Bicycle Relief. (2021). https://worldbicyclerelief.org/dairy-farmer-goes-stronger-with-his-buffalo-bicycle/

Dawadi, S., Shrestha, S., & Giri, R. A. (2021). Mixed-Methods Research: A Discussion on its Types, Challenges, and Criticisms. *Journal of Practical Studies in Education*, *2*(2). https://doi.org/: https://doi.org/10.46809/jpse.v2i2.20

Dos Anjos Luis, A., & Cabral, P. (2016). *Geographic accessibility to primary healthcare centers in Mozambique*. *15*(1), 1–13. https://doi.org/10.1186/s12939-016-0455-0

Easterbrook, S., Singer, J., Storey, M.-A., & Damian, D. (2008). *Selecting Empirical Methods for Software Engineering Research* (pp. 285–311). doi:10.1007/978-1-84800-044-5_11

Enkhtuya, D., & Shin, K. (2019). Designing the Optimal Urban Distribution Network Using Gis: Case of Milk Industry in Ulaanbaatar Mongolia. *The Journal of Bigdata, Volume 4*(Issue 2), 159–173.

Fazal, S. (2008). *GIS Basics*. New Age International (P) Limited.

Floch, J., Marcon, E., & Puech, F. (2018). *Spatial Distribution of Points*. https://ericmarcon.github.io/en/publication/floch-2018-a/

Flowerdew, R., & Stillwell, J. (2004). *Applied GIS and Spatial Analysis*. John Wiley & Sons Ltd,.

Fussi, J. I. (2010). *Strategies to increase milk deliveries to the Tanzanian milk processing industry: A case of ASAS Dairies Ltd in Iringa district*. Larenstein University of Applied Sciences-Part of Wageningen University.

Garrard, C. (2016). *Geoprocessing with Python*. Manning Publications Co.

Grant, A., & Osanloo, C. (2014). *Understanding, Selecting, and Integrating a Theoretical Framework in Dissertation Research: Creating the Blueprint for 'House' Administrative Issues Journal: Connecting Education, Practice and Research, pp. 12-22*. https://doi.org/DOI: 10.5929/2014.4.2.9

Guerin, B. (2019). The Use of Participatory and Non-Experimental Research Methods in Behavior Analysis. *Perspectivas Em Análise Do Comportamento*, *9*(2), 248–264. https://doi.org/10.18761/PAC.2018.n2.09

Hansson, S. O. (2005). *Decision Theory A Brief Introduction*.

Illian, J., Penttinen, A., Stoyan, H., & Stoyan, D. (2008). *Statistical Analysis and Modelling of Spatial Point Patterns*. John Wiley & Sons Ltd,.

Imani Development Consultants. (2004). Review of the Dairy Industry in Malawi. *Final Report Prepared for RATES.*

Kariithi, D. M. (2008). *Application of GPS and GIS in Dairy Livestock Management: Case Study of Mt. Kenya Region*. University of Nairobi.

Kennedy, M., & Kopp, S. (2000). *Understanding Map Projections*.

Kharel, S., & Shivananda, D. (2018). Transportation network model for route and closest facility analysis in central Bengaluru. *IJAIEM*, *7*(4), 58–62.

Kivunja, C. (2018). *Distinguishing between Theory, Theoretical Framework, and Conceptual Framework: A Systematic Review of Lessons from the Field*. *7*(6). https://doi.org/doi:10.5430/ijhe.v7n6p44

Kumar, A., Kumar, R., & Rao, K. H. (2012). Enabling Efficient Supply Chain in Dairying Using GIS: A Case of Private Dairy Industry in Andhra Pradesh State. *India Journal of Agriculture Economics*, *67*(Number 3).

Lall, S. V., Wang, H., & Munthali, T. (2009). *Explaining High Transport Costs within Malawi-Bad Roads or Lack of Trucking Competition?*

Leavy, P. (2017). *Quantitative, Qualitative, Mixed Methods, Arts-Based, and Community-Based Participatory Research Approaches*. The Guilford Press.

Lim, S., Saldanha, T., Malladi, S., & Melville, N. P. (2009). Theories Used in Information Systems Research: Identifying Theory Networks in Leading IS Journals. *International Conference on Information Systems (ICIS)*, *91*. http://aisel.aisnet.org/icis2009/91

Lucas-Cuevas, A. G., Pérez-Soriano, P., Bush, M., Crossman, A., Llana, S., Cortell-Tormo, J. M., & Pérez-Turpin, J. A. (2013). Effects of Different Backpack Loads in Acceleration Transmission during Recreational Distance Walking. *Journal of Human Kinetics*, *37*, 81–89. https://doi.org/10.2478/hukin-2013-0028

Mansour, S. (2016). *Spatial Analysis of Public Health Facilities in Riyadh Governorate, Saudi Arabia: A GIS-Based Study to Assess Geographic Variations of Service Provision and Accessibility* [Alexandria University]. http://dx.doi.org/10.1080/10095020.2016.1151205

McKinney, W. (2012). *Python for data analysis: Data wrangling with Pandas, NumPy, and IPython*. O'Reilly Media, Inc.

M-Livestock Consultant. (2013). *Dairy Value Chain Mapping & Analysis*.

M-Livestock Consultant. (2016). *Assessment of Milk Processors' Absorption Capacity in Malawi*.

Montoya-Torres, J. R., López Franco, J., Nieto Isaza, S., Felizzola Jiménez, H., & Herazo-Padilla, N. (2015). A literature review on the vehicle routing problem with multiple depots. *Computers & Industrial Engineering*, *79*, 115–129. https://doi.org/10.1016/j.cie.2014.10.029

Mulcahy, K. A., & Clarke, K. C. (2001). *Symbolization of Map Projection Distortion: A Review*. *28*(3), 167–182. http://dx.doi.org/10.1559/152304001782153044

Nagrale, S. D., Khedkar, S., Rangdal, A., Patil, S., & Patil, A. (2018). *Route Optimization of Solid Waste by using ArcGIS Application in Pune, India*. *4*.

Ngigi, M. M., & Wangai, L. M. (2012). *GIS in Logistics and Transportation for a Dairy Co-Operative Society in Kenya.* https://www.researchgate.net/publication/275209209

NSO, N. S. O. (2018). *2018 Malawi Population and Housing Census Report.*

Nyekanyeka, T. (2011). *Analysis of Profitability and Efficiency of Improved and Local Smallholder Dairy Farmer: A Case of Lilongwe Milk Shed Area.* University of Malawi: Bunda College of Agriculture.

O'Callaghan, S., O'Connor, D., & Goulding, D. (2021). A dynamic decision support model for the seasonal transportation of raw milk. *International Journal of Dairy Technology*, *74*(1), 32–43.

Odland, J. (2020). *Spatial Autocorrelation* (Web Book Version). Sage Publications; WVU Research Repository. https://researchrepository.wvu.edu/cgi/viewcontent.cgi?article=1019&context=rri-web-book

Ommani, A. R., & Chizari, M. (2008). *Information dissemination system (IDS) based e-learning in agricultural of Iran (perception of Iranian extension agents).* 468–472. http://www.waset.org/journals/waset/v38/v38-84.pdf

Otaala, S. (2016). *An assessment of the Extent of ICT Use along the Dairy Value Chain in Western Uganda A.* Haramaya University.

Palk, L., Okano, J. T., Dullie, L., & Blower, S. (2020). *Travel time to health-care facilities, mode of transportation, and HIV elimination in Malawi: A geospatial modelling analysis. 8.*

Parmigiani, G., & Inoue, L. Y. T. (2009). *Decision Theory Principles and Approaches*. John Wiley & Sons, Ltd.

Pascal, B., & Fermat, P. de. (1654). *Fermat & Pascal on Probability*. https://www.york.ac.uk/depts/maths/histstat/pascal.pdf

Price, A. J., Crampin, A. C., Amberbir, A., Kayuni-Chihana, N., Musicha, C., Tafatatha, T., Branson, K., Lawlor, D. A., Mwaiyeghele, E., Nkhwazi, L., Smeeth, L., Pearce, N., Munthali, E., Mwagomba, B. M., Mwansambo, C., Glynn, J. R., Jaffar, S., & Nyirenda, M. (2018). Prevalence of obesity, hypertension, and diabetes, and cascade of care in sub-Saharan Africa: A cross-sectional, population-based study in rural and urban Malawi. *The Lancet Diabetes & Endocrinology*, *6*(3), 208–222. https://doi.org/10.1016/S2213-8587(17)30432-1

Raballand, G., Thornton, R. L., Yang, D., Goldberg, J., Keleher, N. C., & Mueller, A. (2011). *Are Rural Road Investments Alone Sufficient to Generate Transport Flows? Lessons from a Randomized Experiment in Rural Malawi and Policy Implications* (SSRN Scholarly Paper 1747438). Social Science Research Network. https://papers.ssrn.com/abstract=1747438

Rai, P. K., Singh, P. K., Singh, A. K., & Mohan, K. (2005). *Network Analysis Using GIS*. International Journal of Emerging Technologies in Computational and Applied Sciences (IJETCAS).

Rajeev, L., Kumar, P. S., & Rao, S. K. (2015). *Design of Milk Analysis Embedded System for Dairy Farmers*. *07*(09), 1678–1681.

Ratner, B. (2017). *Statistical and machine-learning data mining: Techniques for better predictive modeling and analysis of big data*. CRC Press.

Resnik, D. B. (2015). *What is Ethics in Research & Why is it Important?* National Institute of Environmental Health Sciences. http://nook.cs.ucdavis.edu/~koehl/Teaching/ECS188/Reprints/Ethics_Research_NIH.pdf

Revoredo-Giha, C. (2016). Market Structure and Coherence of International Cooperation: The Case of the Dairy Sector in Malawi. *Agricultural and Food Economic*, *4*(8), 1–23. https://doi.org/DOI 10.1186/s40100-016-0052-y

Revoredo-Giha, C., Arakelyan, I., Chalmers, N., & Chitika, R. (2013, September 22). *How Responsive to Prices is the Supply of Milk in Malawi?* 4th International Conference of the African Association of Agricultural Economists, Hammamet, Tunisia.

Revoredo-Giha, C. L., Jumbe, C. B. L., Glenk, K., Moran, D., Chagunda, M., Renwick, A., Barnes, A., & Toma, L. (2015). *Assessing the Contribution of the Dairy Sector to Economic Growth and Food Security in Malawi*. Scotland Rural College. https://gtr.ukri.org/projects?ref=ES%2FJ009202%2F1#/tabOverview

Revoredo-Giha, C., & Toma, L. (2016, September 23). *Assessing the Development Strategies for the Malawian Dairy Sector: A Spatial Multimarket Model*. Invited paper presented at the 5th International Conference of the African Association of Agricultural Economists, Addis Ababa, Ethiopia.

Route analysis—ArcMap | Documentation. (2021). https://desktop.arcgis.com/en/arcmap/latest/extensions/network-analyst/route.htm

Sahroni, T. R., Anggoro, L. A., Ismail, S., & Aerna. (2018). Application of an Open Source Spreadsheet Solver in Single Depot Routing Problem. *Computers & Operations Research*, *7*(6), 375–381.

Sanjeevi, V., & Shahabudeen, P. (2015). *Optimal routing for efficient municipal solid waste transportation by using ArcGIS application in Chennai, India* [College of Engineering, Anna University,]. DOI: 10.1177/0734242X15607430

Silverman, D. (2017). *Doing Qualitative Research*. SAGE Publications. https://books.google.mw/books?id=2FAlDwAAQBAJ

Sindani, W. G. (2012). *The Dairy Industry in Malawi-A Description of the Milk Bulking Groups in Malawi*. North Carolina State University.

Thill, J.-C. (2009). *Geographic Information Systems in Transportation Research*. Emerald Group Publishing Limited.

Thomson, S., Barnes, A., Chagunda, M., Chitika, R., Chiumia, D., & Kawonga, B. (2020). *Malawi's Milk Bulking Groups*. https://assets.publishing.service.gov.uk/media/57a09dd7e5274a27b2001a83/60974_Malawi_milk_bulking.pdf

Wiggins, S., & Revoredo-Giha, C. (2016). *Dairying in Malawi*. https://assets.publishing.service.gov.uk/media/5c44b41e40f0b6172bad8432/DEGRP-RiC-Dairy-in-Malawi.pdf

Wohlin, C., & Aurum, A. (2015). Towards a decision-making structure for selecting a research design in empirical software engineering. *Empirical Software Engineering*, *20*(6), 1427–1455. https://doi.org/10.1007/s10664-014-9319-7

Worah, D., Paghadar, M., & Mitra, S. (2012). *Milk procurement route optimization using GIS in a farmers' diary Organization.* Annual International Conference and Exhibition on Geospatial Information Technology and Applications.

Xu, L. (2005). *A Decision Support Model Based on GIs for Vehicle Routing.* School of Management, Shanghai Jiao Tong University.

Zohrabi, M. (2013). *Mixed Method Research: Instruments, Validity, Reliability and Reporting Findings* [University of Tabriz,]. https://doi:10.4304/tpls.3.2.254-262

Appendix A: Interview Guide

<u>Interview Guide (Data Collection)</u>

Date:

Time:

Place:

Interviewee:

Method: Face to Face interview

Thematic Areas

- BG details
    - Name:
    - Location/Trading centre:
    - Village:
    - TA:
    - GPS –
        - Latitude (S):
        - Longitude (E):
- Membership
    - Committee:
    - Registered farmers:
        - Dry:
        - Active:
    - Association:
    - Funder:
    - Processor:
- Milk collection and management
    -
- Farmers data management
    -
- Sales management
    -
- Farmer welfare
    -

Appendix B: Study Questionnaire

A. GENERAL DAIRY FARMER'S INFORMATION

1. Milk Bulking Group: --
   ----
2. Village : --
   ----
3. TA : --

B. MILK PRODUCTION

4. How many times do you milk your cow(s) in a day? *Please tick applicable option:*

Once	
Twice	
Thrice	

5. Average milk produced per day during:

Season	**Number of Litres**	**Number of Cows**
Dry		
Rainy		

6. Do you have plans to increase milk production volumes? *Please tick applicable option*

Yes	
No	

6.1 If yes, how do you plan to increase the amount of milk you produce? (*Please tick an applicable option)*

Increase the number of dairy cows	
Change breed of animals	
Provide more feed	

Other...
....

7. Why did you start dairy farming? (*Please tick your response– you can select more than 1 option*)

To increase income	
To diversify sources of income	
To increase food security	

Others, please specify...

C. TRANSPORTATION

8. What mode of transport do you normally use to deliver your milk to the Milk Bulking Group? (*Please tick applicable option)*

Mode of Transport	
On foot	
Bicycle	
Wheelbarrow	
Motorcycle	
Ox-cart	
Vehicle	

- Other (specify)..

8.1 How long does it take to deliver milk from the farm/home to the Milk Bulking

Group? ....Minutes/Hours

8.2 Do you know the distance from your farm/home to the Milk Bulking Group?

Yes	
No	

8.2.1 If you answered yes, how long is the distance?.......................................KM

D. CONSTRAINTS

9. Do you think there are any significant constraints to the (dairy) production at farm level? (*Please tick applicable option)*

Yes	
No	

9.1 If you answered yes, which are the 2 main constraints you are facing (*please tick any applicable options)*

CONSTRAINTS	*(Please tick any)*
Poor quality of milk	
Lack of funding to purchase additional animals	
Low milk production	
Low market price	
Miscalculation of revenue	
Inconsistent collection of milk by processors	
Poor road quality in rainy season	
Poor communication by processors or BG Executives	

Other, please specify ---

10. Do you ever have difficulties selling your milk? *Please tick applicable answer*

Yes	
No	

10.1 If you answered yes, what are the difficulties? Please tick the applicable option?

CONSTRAINTS	*(Please tick any)*
Milk deterioration	
Poor road network	
Lack of market	
Poor transportation	
Low price per litre	

Other, please specify ---

11. How often is your milk rejected in a month (number of times) ----------

12. What volume of your milk in liters was rejected on average by your MBG in the last month?..Litres

13. Do you face delays in getting paid for milk supplied to the Bulking Group?

Yes	
No	

17.1 If yes, how many times has your payment been delayed in the last 12 months? --------------------------

14. In your opinion what do you think are the causes of delays in payment? Please state as many reasons as you can

- ---
- ---

15. As a dairy farmer, are you aware that you contribute to the national economy of Malawi?

Yes	
No	

16. Do you have any other recommendations for improvement of dairy farming in Malawi?

- ---
- ---

The End.

Appendix C: Consent Note

My name is Sunday Nanosi Ndovi and I am a pursuing Master of Science Degree in Informatics at University of Malawi, Chancellor College. As partial fulfillment of the two-year degree program, I am conducting a study concerning milk transportation from farm to Milk Bulking Group using GIS in Thyolo district.

To better understand the present dairy systems, researcher will ask questions on general information, milk production, transportation and constraints that will help in identifying challenges in the industry. Subsequently, this will present improvements to be made and assist in decision making. Information that you give, will be used for academic purposes and help the stakeholders to formulate policies for intensification of computer technology in dairy industry.

You are unlikely to be subjected to any form of risks. However, if you feel that you have become uncomfortable or experience any problems due to your voluntary participation in this research, you may choose to pull out at any time. The participation or withdrawal will not affect any entitlements to your rights. Please note that neither will you incur costs nor receive any payment for your participation in this research study.

Please note that there is no wrong answer. Therefore, you are requested to give your honest opinion. Your identity and answers you give will be treated with utmost confidentiality. The researcher hopes that you will be willing to respond to listed questions.
Should you have queries regarding this research, please feel free to contact the researcher or The Registrar, University of Malawi, Chancellor College, P.O Box 280, Zomba, Telephone +265 (0) 1524222.

Appendix D: Milk Supply Record at bulking Group

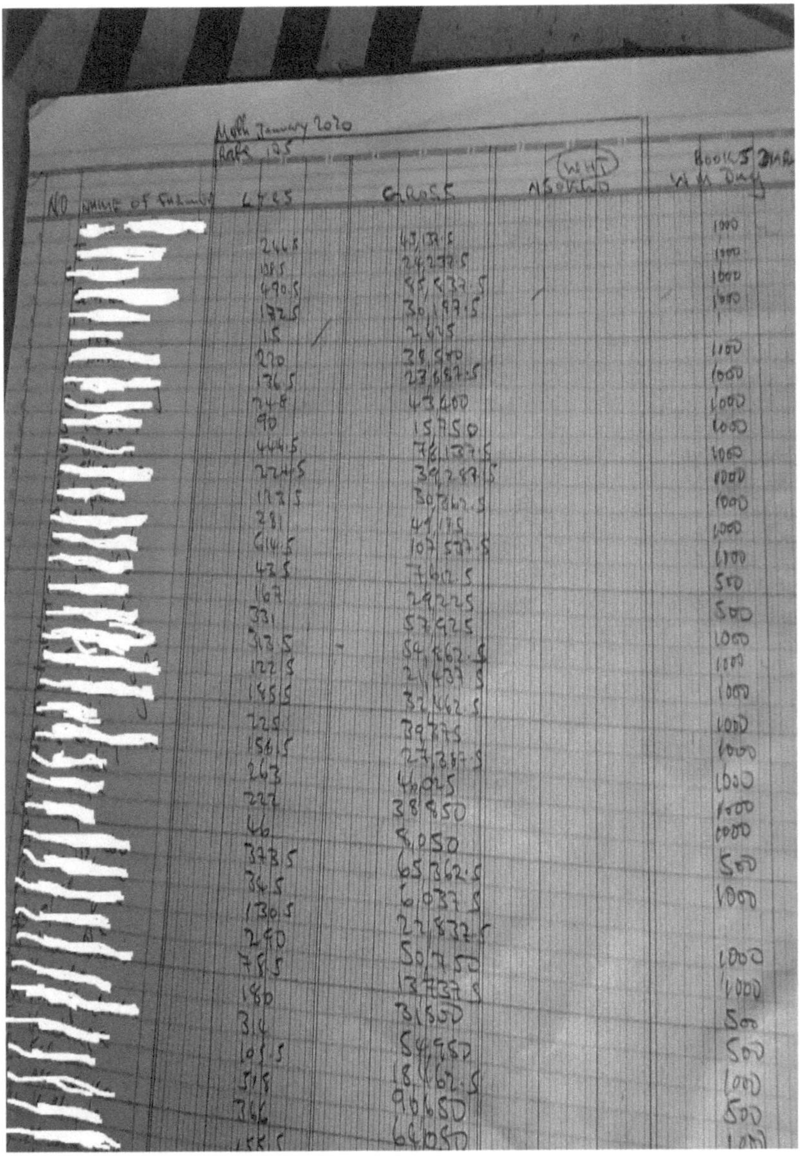

Appendix E: Reference Letter

PRINCIPAL
Richard Tambulasi, B.A (Pub Admin), BPA (Hons), MPA, Ph.D

CHANCELLOR COLLEGE
P.O. Box 280, Zomba, Malawi
Telephone: (265) 524 222
Fax: (265) 524 046
E-mail: principal@cc.ac.mw

TO WHOM IT MAY CONCERN
15 March 2020

REFERENCE FOR MR. SUNDAY NDOVI (MSC/INF/07/18)

As per the subject matter, Mr. Sunday Ndovi, registration number MSC/INF/07/18 is a student at Chancellor College pursuing an MSc in Informatics under the Computer Science Department. He seeks to collect data for his research, titled *Evaluating Logistics of Unprocessed Milk in Malawi: A Spatial Analysis Approach*. Any assistance rendered to him for the same would be greatly appreciated.

Yours faithfully,

Martin Thodi
Programme Coordinator, MSc Informatics
martinthodi@cc.ac.mw – 0883816293

Appendix F: Cover Letter

CHANCELLOR COLLEGE

Sunday Nanosi Ndovi,
University of Malawi,
Chancellor College,
P.O Box 280,
Zomba.
20th April, 2019

To Whom It May Concern

Dear Sir\Madam

REQUEST TO USE YOUR TERRITORY/INSTITUTION AS CASE STUDY

I write to seek permission to use your territory/institution as case study for my Master of Science research entitled "Evaluating Logistics of Unprocessed Milk in Dairy Industry: Spatial Analysis Approach". The study will be purely for academic purposes.

Lastly, I look forward to hearing from you.

Kind Regards,
Sunday Nanosi Ndovi
0999269725 / 0884500858 / msc-inf-07-18@cc.ac.mw

Appendix G: Consent Letter from Blantyre Agricultural Development Division

Ref. No// BLADD/ ADM/2 **11th June 2019**

FROM THE PROGRAMME MANAGER, BLANTYRE ADD
PRIVATE BAG 379, BLANTYRE 3.

CC THE ECONOMIIST, PLANNING DEPARTMENT, BLANTYRE ADD

TO WHOM IT MAY CONCERN

REQUEST FOR STUDENT ATTACHMENT

This is to certify that **SUNDAY NDOVI**, a student at Chancellor College studying Master of Science Degree in Informatics has been authorized to carry out his research at this office starting from 1st July, 2019 to 31st July 2020 (**1 full year**).

Any assistance rendered to him will be greatly appreciated.

Eunice Nakoma

For: **PROGRAMME MANAGER.**

Appendix H: Consent Letter from Shire Highlands Milk Producers Association

PO Box 30603
Blantyre
Malawi
Tel. 673 352

Shire Highlands Milk Producers Assoc.

May 7, 2019

Sunday N. Ndovie
University of Malawi
P.O. Box 280
Zomba

Dear Sir:

Re: REQUEST OF USE SHMPA AS A CASE STUDY IN MY MASTERS' THESIS

Thank you for the letter dated 20th April 2019, in which you seek permission to use our territory as the case study.

We are here to give you a go ahead but remember to go through the bulking group committee.

Yours faithfully,

S. Kapito,

Deputy Chairman General – SHMPA.

Appendix I: Consent Letter from Dairibord Malawi Limited

DAIRIBORD MALAWI LIMITED

DAIRIBORD MALAWI
P.O. Box 30647
Chichiri, Blantyre 3, Malawi
Tel: (265) 1 871 450 / 1 871 561
(265) 1 870 475
Fax: (265) 1 870 258
Website: www.dairibord.com

20 March 2019

Mr S Ndovi
C/o University of Malawi
Chancellor College
P O Box 280
ZOMBA

Dear Sunday

REQUEST TO USE DAIRIBORD MALAWI LIMITED AS A CASE STUDY IN MASTERS THESIS

Reference is made to the above and your letter dated 28 February 2019 wherein you requested to use Dairibord Malawi Limited as a case study in partial fulfilment of your Masters of Science Degree in Informatics.

We write to advise that you request has been approved and consent given for you to use Dairibord Malawi Limited as a case study. This approval has been given on condition that you will share your findings and a copy of your final document to the organisation to be used for continuous improvement.

We wish you the best in your studies.

Yours sincerely
For & On Behalf of Dairibord Malawi Limited

MARGARET CHIROMBE
HUMAN RESOURCES MANAGER

Appendix J: Farms and Milk Bulking Groups in Thyolo district on Google Maps

https://www.google.com/maps/d/u/0/viewer?mid=10HyEMlfLXkfiqIfQyhorgaUlcjpbR88&ll=-15.966330560150416%2C35.1589865285 1235&z=12

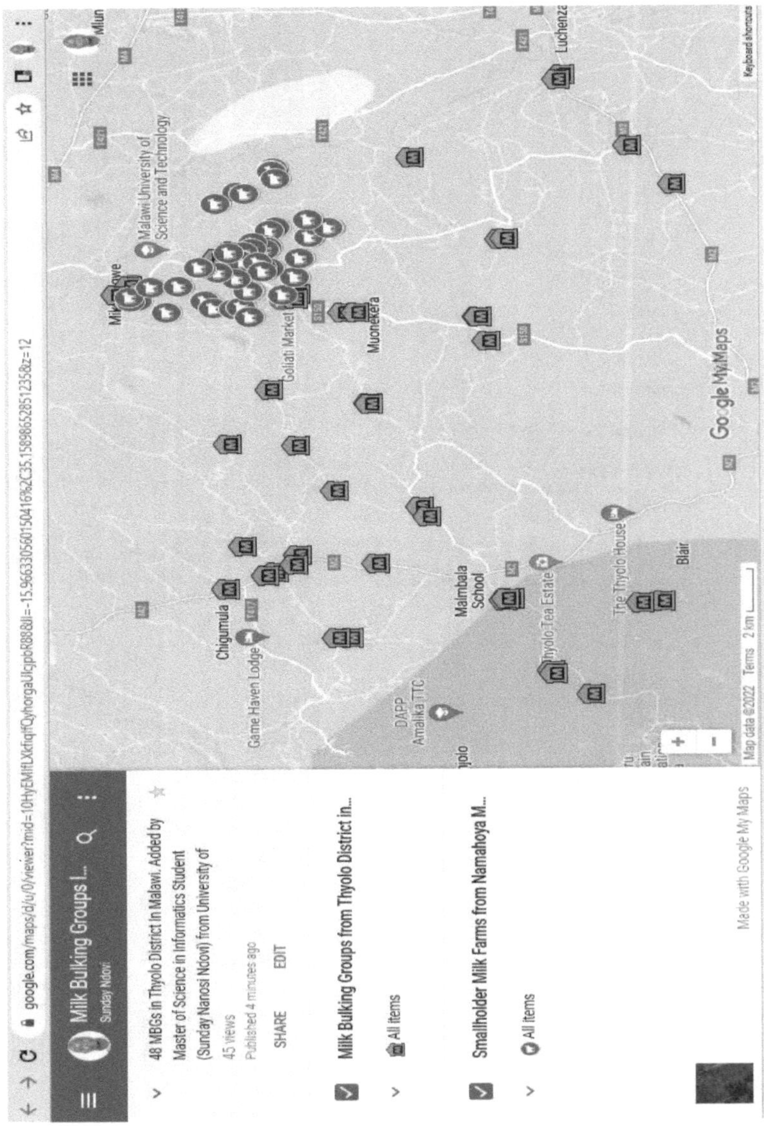

Kolibri 360 GmbH
Ferdinand-Jühlke-Straße 7
99095 Erfurt, Deutschland
produktsicherheit@kolibri360.de

Druck:
CPI Druckdienstleistungen GmbH
im Auftrag der
Kolibri 360 GmbH
Ferdinand-Jühlke-Str. 7
99095 Erfurt